AUTISM

INFORMATION AND RESOURCES FOR PARENTS, FAMILIES, AND PROFESSIONALS

RICHARD L. SIMPSON

PAUL ZIONTS

pro·ed

8700 Shoal Creek Boulevard
Austin, Texas 78757

© 1992 by PRO-ED, Inc.

Printed in the United States of America

Library of Congress Cataloging-in-Publication Data

Simpson, Richard L., 1945–
    Autism: information and resources for parents, families and
professionals / Richard L. Simpson, Paul Zionts.
        p.   cm.
    Includes bibliographical references.
    ISBN 0–89079–538–X
    1. Autism—Popular works.   I. Zionts, Paul.   II. Title.
RJ506.A9S56   1992
618.92′8982—dc20   92-1
                                                        CIP

pro·ed

8700 Shoal Creek Boulevard
Austin, Texas 78757

2   3   4   5   6   7   8   9   10   96   95

Contents

*To Janice and Dottie: Good friends are
hard to find.*

Preface

This book is primarily written for parents and family members who directly experience the frustration, concern, and uncertainty of living with a youngster with autism. Thus, while the information is scientifically valid, it is presented in such a manner that parents and other lay persons will understand it without difficulty.

In question-answer format, we attempt to answer common questions about autism. We have selected questions asked of us by countless parents and family members of children and youth with autism. These individuals continually ask the same type of questions: What is autism? What causes autism? Did we do something to cause our child to develop autism? Is there a cure for autism? What can we do to help someone who has autism? What will become of a child with autism when he or she is an adult? Why does our child continually flap his arms and do other bizarre things?

A myriad of questions surround autism; for some of them we have answers. For others, there are no definitive answers. In such cases, we have summarized and discussed what is known and reported the progress being made to better understand and deal with a particular issue.

Autism was first described in the medical literature nearly 50 years ago. Since that time a great deal has been learned about the disorder. In fact, we have literally witnessed an explosion of knowledge and information about children and youth with autism; as a result, many individuals with the disorder are now experiencing successes that earlier would have been considered nearly impossible. Children and adolescents with autism have also benefited from the commitment and perseverance of parents and families, and the willingness of schools, communities, and legislators to commit resources in behalf of these citizens. It is our belief that the future will continue to open doors for individuals with autism if professionals, parents, communities, and decision makers are well informed. It is with this mission in mind that this book was written.

1

Introduction to Autism and Pervasive Developmental Disorders

Children and youth diagnosed as having *autism* and *pervasive developmental disorders* have received considerable attention in recent years. Dustin Hoffman skillfully portrayed Raymond, a high-functioning adult with autism in the movie *Rainman;* the National Football League Charities have established autism information libraries; magazines and newspapers have published countless human-interest stories about individuals with autism; and TV specials have brought the subject of autism into American homes. Such attention has created strong interest in autism and pervasive developmental disorders; yet, the complexity of these disorders leaves us with many unanswered questions (e.g., Exactly what is autism? How many individuals have autism?).

This book is primarily designed for parents and family members of children with autism, persons interested in learning more about autism, and professionals who may have occasional contact with children and youth with autism. Thus, it is intended for "nonexperts" in the field of autism (a number of books and periodicals on autism focus on the information needs of professionals). Without going into great depth, we attempt to give readers an overview of concepts and characteristics of autism; background on the disorder; and alternatives, considerations, and strategies for obtaining education, treatment, and support.

1

The book primarily focuses on children and adolescents. While we recognize that autism affects individuals of all ages, and that families and care givers of adults with autism also need information and strategies for meeting the unique challenges they face, we have directed our attention on young people with autism. In so doing, we are able to provide maximally relevant information.

Because there is no known cure for autism and because education and training are the cornerstones of autistic children's growth and development, the book emphasizes educational considerations. That is, because children and youth with autism are receiving more and more services from schools and other educational agencies, these programs are increasingly being identified as responsible for children's gains. Accordingly, we give considerable attention to matters of education and training, while at the same time discussing issues related to noneducation professionals, disciplines, and treatments (e.g., mental health, medical interventions, job counseling).

Children and youth with autism are known by different names, including *pervasive developmental disorder, autistic-like* and *higher functioning autism disorder.* We identify these terms (and discuss the somewhat confusing and variable terminology used to describe children with autism); however, for purposes of brevity and convenience we use the term *autism* to refer to children who demonstrate any one of a number of autism-related conditions.

What is meant by "autism"?

Leo Kanner wrote an article in 1943 about 11 children he had seen in his psychiatric practice over the course of several years. These children demonstrated a variety of unique symptoms and behaviors, including desire for sameness (e.g., agitation and distress following changes in their routine or environment), abnormal speech and language development (e.g., speech delays, speech restricted to echoing what others say) and social withdrawal (e.g., extreme preference for aloneness). Kanner observed that these children's behavior generally differed from anything that psychologists and psychiatrists had previously reported. In his seminal article, Kanner used the word *autistic* to describe the children's inability to relate and their strong preference for being left alone. Prior to Kanner, the term *autistic* had been used to refer to a thought-process disorder in persons with schizophrenia, a severe emotional disorder characterized by disturbances of thought, mood, and behavior. Some professionals currently use the term *pervasive developmental disorder* to refer to autism.

Information about autism has dramatically increased since the publication of Kanner's article; however, a number of his observations about the characteristics of children with autism are still current, including: (a) problems in relating normally to people and situations; (b) speech and language problems; (c) developmental delays; (d) problems in reacting to environmental changes; and (e) stereotypic, repetitive actions, and other peculiar motor movements.

What is the difference between "autism" and "pervasive developmental disorders"?

A term commonly used by psychiatrists and psychologists to refer to children and adolescents with autism is *pervasive developmental disorder.* The term is taken from the *Diagnostic and Statistical Manual of Mental Disorders* (3rd ed., revised, 1987), a guide used by mental-health professionals to classify, diagnose, and communicate about mental disorders.

The *Diagnostic and Statistical Manual of Mental Disorders* notes that the term *pervasive developmental disorder* is reserved for children who show problems in a number of basic areas of psychological development at the same time and to a severe degree. Autism is the only specific and most severe form of pervasive developmental disorder.

Children who show signs of pervasive developmental disorder but lack the specific characteristics of autism are classified as having *pervasive developmental disorder not otherwise specified.* In the past, these persons were commonly referred to as *autistic-like;* today a more common term is *higher functioning autistic disorder.*

What is meant by "problems in a number of basic areas of psychological development at the same time and to a severe degree"?

Children with autism have difficulty in relating normally to people and situations, in developing and using speech and language, and in dealing with changes in the environment. Besides, they display nonuseful repetitive actions and other peculiar motor movements. Children with autism also commonly evidence developmental delays (slowness in acquiring skills and developmental milestones).

What is meant by "problems in relating to people and situations"?

Many children and youth with autism experience difficulty in relating and interacting with people. In some instances, they prefer to spend time in isolation or give the appearance of having little awareness or interest in others, including family members. Some parents of children with autism even wonder if their child can hear, based on observations that the child may be oblivious to the presence of others. In other instances, autistic children may attempt to interact with others, in abnormal or unacceptable ways. For example, a child may sniff or lick the ankles or legs of people with whom he comes in contact; or an adolescent may repeatedly ask the same question (e.g., "What is your name?"; "What are you doing?"), ignoring the answer and any cues that it is inappropriate to repeat the same question over and over.

Social interaction problems may also take the form of eye-contact avoidance and reluctance to be near people, particularly strangers. Even higher functioning autistic persons (including children and adolescents) can be expected to have difficulty in developing and maintaining close friendships outside their family and are frequently thought of as socially odd.

To what extent do children and youth with autism have speech and language problems and how significant are these problems?

As noted earlier, speech and language problems are common among children and youth with autism; in fact, a number of experts think that speech and language disorders are the most significant problems of children with autism. In this regard, *speech* refers to forming and using the sounds of oral language (i.e., problems in voice pitch, loudness, or quality disorders; making and using correct speech sounds; and stuttering), while *language,* a broader term, refers to a system or set of rules used by people to communicate. Language problems include absence or delays of verbal language development (i.e., ability to understand and use language); echolalia (parroting back whatever is heard, without saying anything else); nonsense word and sentence use (use of "words" and phrases that have no meaning to others and are not designed to communicate); ineffective use of communication gestures and affect (e.g., poor use of facial expression, gestures, and tone); pronoun reversals (e.g., use of "you" when "I" is intended); inability to name objects; and general difficulty in communicating. Speech and language problems are discussed in detail in a later section of this book.

An estimated one-half of individuals diagnosed as having autism fail to develop spoken language. Even when persons with autism develop speech they typically have difficulty communicating. In fact, language problems are so pervasive that prognosis (prediction about the course and outcome of the disorder) has been related to whether or not persons with autism develop spoken language.

What is meant by "problems of reacting to changes in the environment"?

This common characteristic of children with autism is related to their insistence on sameness. That is, some children with autism may become upset (e.g., tantrum, withdraw, or become aggressive) if their environment is varied. For instance, some parents have reported that their autistic children will only eat or drink from one particular dish or cup; other children have been observed to become agitated if a road detour forces their school bus to take a different route. Every autistic child or adolescent is not adversely affected by environmental changes, however such a pattern is common.

In a related manner, children and youth with autism may demonstrate strong attachment to unusual objects, preferring to maintain contact with the item at all times. For example, a child may keep a single blade of grass or piece of string and become agitated or aggressive if the item is removed. In comparison, nonhandicapped children spontaneously show affection and attachment toward toys and objects (e.g., teddy bears and dolls are valued by many children); however, the items to which they become attached usually have symbolic significance (e.g., a doll has human characteristics, a blanket serves to warm and comfort). The type of object to which autistic and nonhandicapped children become attached, the degree to which they insist upon maintaining contact with an item, and the age of children engaging in such behavior differentiate "normal" from unusual object attachment.

What is meant by "displays of nonuseful repetitive actions and other peculiar motor movements"?

Among the most unusual and puzzling characteristics of children and adolescents with autism is their display of repetitive, stereotypic body movements that appear to have no useful function. These patterns, often referred to as *self-stimulatory behavior,* are designed to provide sensory stimulation. Examples of self-stimulatory behaviors are discussed in Chapter 4.

Self-stimulation can take a nearly infinite number of forms: body rocking, hand flapping, finger waving, light filtering (i.e., child reflects light by moving his hands back and forth in front of his eyes), object twirling, hand rubbing, and a myriad of other behaviors that appear to have no functional value. Some children with autism would spend (if allowed) virtually every waking moment engaged in self-stimulatory behavior, thus interfering with the development of more functional skills. Moreover, self-stimulation is a solitary activity, making it difficult for children to interact with others at the same time. Decreasing self-stimulatory behaviors and replacing these responses with more functional behaviors is often a priority for children with autism.

What types of developmental delays do children and youth with autism demonstrate?

Children's development falls into three primary areas: cognition, social-adaptation, and motor. *Developmental delay* refers to autistic children's tendency to be slower in developing skills, compared to normally developing children; failure to develop particular skills or functions (arrests); or developing and then losing a particular cognitive, social-adaptive, and/or motor skill or function (regression).

Cognitive delays (i.e., intellectual and learning deficits and problems) are typical of children and youth with autism. This does not mean that all children with autism are mentally retarded; on the contrary, some autistic persons have average or above-average intelligence and learning potential. However, the vast majority of children with autism demonstrate intellectual and learning problems.

Problems of social adaptation implies social withdrawal and social deficits. Thus, children and youth with autism can be expected to experience problems in relating to others. This form of developmental delay creates obvious problems for both children and their families.

Children and youth with autism may also show motor delays and deficits (*motor* refers to use of muscles of the body, such as in walking, crawling, writing, etc.). However, motor problems are not as common and pervasive as cognitive and social delays, and some children with autism experience relatively normal motor development.

What kinds of behaviors lead parents to think that their children may have autism?

The following list of characteristics of autism (Rendel-Short, 1978) serves as a helpful guide to common behaviors among children with autism. Not all of these characteristics will necessarily be shown by all children with autism, however they do serve as a valuable checklist.

- experiences difficulty mixing with other children

- acts deaf

- resists learning

- shows no fear of real dangers

- resists change in routine

- indicates needs by gestures

- engages in inappropriate laughing or giggling

- is not cuddly

- shows marked physical activity

- shows limited eye contact

- forms inappropriate attachments to objects

- spins objects

- engages in odd play

- is standoffish

The diagnostic criteria for autistic disorder listed in *The Diagnostic and Statistical Manual of the American Psychiatric Association (III–Revised)* are another valuable source. This guide lists 16 diagnostic items, of which at least 8 must be present (including at least two items from categories A–C) to justify a diagnosis of autism. It is important to note that the behaviors must start during infancy or childhood and that criteria are met only if a behavior is abnormal for an individual's developmental level. For example, infants babble prior to developing spoken language; however, babbling is usually considered abnormal for most older children.

AUTISM CRITERIA OF THE DIAGNOSTIC AND STATISTICAL MANUAL OF THE AMERICAN PSYCHIATRIC ASSOCIATION (III–REVISED)*

A: Social interaction impairments, as demonstrated by:

1. marked lack of awareness of the existence or feelings of others

2. no or abnormal seeking of comfort at times of distress

3. no or impaired imitation

4. no or abnormal social play

5. gross impairment in ability to make peer friendships

B: Communication and imagination impairments, as demonstrated by:

1. no mode of communication

2. markedly abnormal nonverbal communication

3. absence of imaginative activity

4. marked abnormalities in the production of speech

5. marked abnormalities in the form or content of speech (e.g., echoing what has been said, comments that are unrelated to conversations)

6. marked impairment in the ability to initiate or sustain a conversation

C: Limited interests and activities, as demonstrated by:

1. stereotyped body movements

2. preoccupation with objects

3. marked distress over environmental changes

4. unreasonable insistence on following routines

5. markedly restricted range of interests and preoccupation with one narrow interest

---

*Items from *The Diagnostic and Statistical Manual of the American Psychiatric Association (III–Revised)* (pp. 38–39).

Is autism a form of emotional disturbance?

Children with autism share some similarities with other groups of handicapped children, including those with emotional disturbance and behavior disorders. However, *autism is not a form of emotional disturbance*. In fact, The Individuals with Disabilities Education Act, a federal law that has been described as a Bill of Rights for the Handicapped and the primary enactment for structuring educational policy and guaranteeing the rights of handicapped children, specifically excludes students with autism from being categorized as emotionally disturbed. Moreover, the problems experienced by most children and adolescents with behavior disorders and emotional disturbance (e.g., defiance, impulsivity, poor social skills) are quite different from those of persons with autism.

The terms *schizophrenia* and *psychosis* (severe forms of emotional disturbance characterized by thought, mood and behavior disorders, and lack of contact with reality) were once used interchangeably with autism. However, research has determined that autism is different from schizophrenia and psychotic conditions. As a result, most professionals no longer use the terms synonymously.

At what age do children develop autism?

Autism is a lifelong disorder that begins in childhood. Most children with autism show signs of the disorder by 2–3 years of age. In fact, many children with autism are described by their parents as "different" from other children from the time they are born. Parents have observed that even as infants their children were aloof and withdrawn and that often they displayed little concern for others.

Some children with autism appear to develop normally for several years, except for relatively minor problems such as language delays, before showing significant signs of autism. Thus, these children are thought to develop normally for 12 to 24 months, after which time they may display self-stimulatory behavior and lose previously acquired skills, such as speech, social interest, play abilities, and bowel and bladder control.

How many children develop autism?

Autism is a relatively rare disorder. It is estimated that the disorder occurs approximately 4 to 5 times per 10,000 births. When less severe forms of the disorder are included (i.e., children showing some autistic characteristics, but lacking elements of the full syndrome), the incidence increases to about 10 to 15 per 10,000. About 3 or 4 times more boys are diagnosed with autism than girls.

What causes autism?

The exact cause or causes of autism has not been determined. Most experts, however, have concluded that autism occurs as a result of biological conditions. *Biological* (or biophysical) refers to physical factors (i.e., those within a person), including biochemical imbalances, neurological (brain) damage, genetic accidents, and so on.

In contrast, *environmental causes* (i.e., a general term referring to anything external to a child, such as parent attitudes, home experiences, family relationships, school experiences, socioeconomic conditions, community attitudes, etc.) are generally not believed to play a prominent role in the development of autism. While such factors may contribute to a child's educational and treatment program success, experts generally agree that they do not cause autism.

Do parents cause their children to become autistic?

At one time some experts believed that parents were the cause of childhood autism. Specifically, it was thought that parents who were cold, aloof, and distant, or who otherwise had psychological or personality abnormalities, caused their children to become autistic. Thus, in past decades, terms such as "refrigerator mother" were common. Research has clearly shown, however, that children with autism do not all have parents with similar personalities or that parents are the reason for children developing autism. Clearly, *parents are not the cause of autism.* However, parents and families can determine, to a significant degree, the extent to which their children with autism develop and acquire skills and abilities. Thus, children of parents who seek early intervention and who participate in treatment and educational programs tend to make the most significant progress.

Is it true that most children with autism have special talents and abilities?

A small percentage of persons with autism demonstrate unique skills and abilities. For instance, some children have shown the ability to solve advanced mathematical problems without the assistance of a calculator; to reproduce songs on a musical instrument they have heard only a single time; to memorize difficult and lengthy materials; and to otherwise show skills that are inconsistent with their overall abilities and functioning level.

Only a small percentage of children and youth with autism show special abilities, however. Moreover, the skills shown by these children and youth often have minimal functional value. For example, a child may be able to accurately calculate, in his head, the answer to difficult division problems, but be unable to make change for a dollar.

Is it true that children with autism are usually attractive and experience no problems in addition to autism?

Many children with autism appear "normal," and some are considered to be exceptionally attractive. That is, unlike many moderately and severely handicapped persons, children with autism may not show any physical signs of their disability. Consequently, casual observations of children with autism may not reveal any abnormalities. However, even individuals who know little about autism will be able to identify children with autism as exceptional if allowed to interact and observe their behavior.

A percentage of children with autism will demonstrate other disabilities in addition to autism, including Down's Syndrome, deafness, and visual impairments. Moreover, the probability of children having autism and autistic-like characteristics increases when they have certain other conditions, including phenylketonuria (PKU) (an inherited condition that may result in brain damage and severe mental retardation), encephalitis (inflammation of the brain that may cause brain damage and mental retardation), meningitis (inflammation of the brain or spinal cord), and tubular sclerosis (genetic disease associated with convulsive seizures and mental retardation).

Can children and youth with autism be educated?

Children and youth with autism can and do benefit from education and training. While curriculum and procedures will vary depending on individual needs, *all children and youth diagnosed as having autism require and benefit from education and training.*

Some children with autism are educated in regular classrooms. Others may require special education services designed for students with mild learning and social handicaps, such as those for pupils who have learning disabilities. Still other children and youth diagnosed as having autism may require a special education program designated specifically for autistic or moderately/severely handicapped pupils. These programs vary in structure, curriculum, and procedures; however, they have all consistently shown that they can make significant positive contributions to the lives of children and youth with autism.

What happens to autistic children and youth when they become adults? Are they easily cured?

There is no known cure for autism. Thus, children diagnosed as having autism will likely evidence at least some characteristics of the syndrome throughout their life. This does not mean that children and youth with autism cannot and do not make substantial gains and improvements; they do. However, even children who make substantial improvements will likely show some remnants of autism, such as social ineptitude, preference for solitude, and so on, even as adults.

It is difficult to say what will become of a child diagnosed as having autism due to the various symptoms associated with the syndrome and the variance in the degree of impairment. Children with relatively normal intelligence who have useful language tend to achieve the best outcomes. Moreover, children who are treated by well-trained professionals representing multiple disciplines, including education, speech/language, medicine, psychology, parent/family support, occupational/physical therapy, vocational and community living, tend to have the best success.

The American Psychiatric Association, in 1980, estimated that approximately one autistic child in six could be expected to achieve marginal social adjustment, competitive employment, and live independently as an adult. Further, the American Psychiatric Association estimated that another one in six persons with autism is able to live semi-independently (i.e., needs assistance in meeting the demands of everyday life), while approximately two-thirds remain severely handicapped and unable to live independently. With increased opportunities for early intervention, improved educational and training programs, supportive employment programs for persons with disabilities, and community living programs (e.g., group homes), the long-term independent living outlook for persons with autism appears to be improving.

Is it true that children with autism have similar socioeconomic, cultural, and ethnic backgrounds?

Autism does not primarily occur in persons from any one socioeconomic, racial, cultural, ethnic, or other group. Children from wealthy families and poor families; children who are black, white, Native American, oriental, Jewish, Baptist, and who are members of every other conceivable subgroup may develop autism. Moreover, autism has been observed to occur in every country and region of the world.

How are children diagnosed as autistic?

Three primary areas of functioning are usually considered when determining if a child has autism. First, children with autism fail to develop age-appropriate interpersonal relationships and tend to be unresponsive or abnormal in their responses and interactions with other people. As discussed earlier, this pattern of behavior may take a variety of forms (e.g., avoidance of eye contact, avoidance of people, difficulty mixing with other children).

A second consideration in diagnosing autism is language. Some children with autism fail to develop spoken language; however, even if less severe, virtually all children diagnosed as having autism have speech and communication problems. As noted earlier, communication and speech problems take the form of language delays, echolalia, utterance of nonsense sounds, ineffective use of gestures, and other communication abnormalities. These problems are discussed in a later section of the book.

Finally, children considered for a diagnosis of autism are evaluated on the basis of their behavior. Particular attention is given to (a) insistence on sameness (e.g., a child insists on the window blinds in his home being kept at precisely the same angle); (b) peculiar object attachment (e.g., child insists on always having in her possession a particular piece of small string); (c) self-stimulatory and other unusual repetitive motor responses (e.g., body rocking, hand flapping); (d) odd play (e.g., spinning objects for long periods of time); and (e) inappropriate laughing or other emotional responses occurring independent of events typically associated with such responses (e.g., child laughs for extended periods of time for no apparent reason).

Three additional factors are also considered when children are evaluated for autism: *intensity, pattern,* and *duration* of behavior. *Intensity* refers to the severity of a child's problem or problems. For example, does a child rock with such intensity that it makes him appear extremely odd, or is his self-stimulation a very subtle behavior, such as slightly moving a finger? Intensity also relates to the degree to which a response interferes with a child's ability to function. Obviously, a behavior that disrupts a child's ability to do other things is more significant than one that does not.

Pattern refers to the times when the problems occur. For example, does a child repeat nonsense words at home, but use functional language at school? Does a child interact in an age-appropriate fashion at home or in his neighborhood but have poor relationships at school? Does a child engage in self-stimulatory hand waving only when she is tired? Answers to these questions are basic to making an accurate diagnosis of autism.

Duration refers to the length of time a child's problems last. For example, the body-rocking behavior of a child who rocks for a short time (e.g., few weeks) subsequent to a family crisis (e.g., divorce, death of a parent) is viewed differently than for a child who has been rocking since birth.

Children evaluated for autism should be assessed by a group of professionals (referred to as *multidisciplinary evaluation teams*) representing several areas of expertise (known as comprehensive evaluations). Autism is a complex disability that affects a number of areas of psychological development. Thus, diagnoses of autism should not be made by a single professional. Moreover, evaluations should consider a number of areas of development (e.g., motor, cognitive, behavior, speech/language, social). Only such evaluations (referred to as *multidisciplinary* and *comprehensive*) are able to accurately and effectively identify children with autism.

Are other terms used to describe children with autism, in addition to "autism" and "pervasive developmental disorder"?

One such term is *developmental disability.* The term refers to a disability of a person that (a) is attributable to a mental and/or physical impairment; (b) occurs prior to age 22; (c) is likely to continue indefinitely; (d) results in significant limitations in self-care, language, learning, mobility, self-direction, independent living or economic self-sufficiency (at least three of the above must be affected); and (e) requires specialized care that is lifelong or of extended duration and that is individually planned and coordinated.

Developmental disability is a general term used to describe individuals with a variety of conditions, including mental retardation, cerebral palsy and autism. Thus, some professionals may use the term instead of more specific terms such as autism.

SUMMARY

The purpose of this chapter was to provide the reader with a general overview of autism and pervasive developmental disorders. Each of the topics discussed (along with related topics) is dealt with in greater detail in later sections of this book.

Causes of Autism and the Effects of Environmental Factors on the Behavior of Children and Youth with Autism

It is only natural to want to identify a cause for human abnormalities, disabilities, and unusual behavior. When we encounter a child in a wheelchair or an individual with an obvious disability, an initial reaction is to wonder why and how such conditions develop. Thus, it is understandable that parents, family members, teachers, relatives, friends, and the general public want to know the cause or causes of autism.

Precise and definitive causes of autism are rarely known. However, more is being learned about the reasons for autism all the time. At the same time, myths and inaccurate notions about the causes of autism are being challenged and replaced with more valid and factual information.

What myths and beliefs regarding causes of autism are being challenged?

Dr. Leo Kanner observed several common family characteristics of the group of autistic children he described in 1943. Specifically, he noted that the parents of the children were for the most part highly intelligent;

17

many were professionals; they appeared to be preoccupied with artistic, literary, and scientific matters; and all were thought to be somewhat cold and aloof (e.g., Kanner noted that there were ". . . few really warmhearted fathers and mothers" [p. 249]). As a result of Kanner's observations, a number of professionals incorrectly assumed that all parents of children with autism were cold and aloof and that such personality characteristics were primary causes of autism. Further, some psychiatrists, psychologists, and other professionals went so far as to recommend that children with autism be separated from their parents at an early age as a means of enhancing their chances of progress.

It is now known that *not* all parents and family members of children with autism are cold and aloof. The parents of children with autism display a range of personalities and dispositions (e.g., some parents are outgoing, some are reserved). Moreover, even in instances where parents may be somewhat aloof, such personality characteristics are not the cause of autism.

Autism has also been shown to exist in all cultures, races, societies, and subgroups. Thus, autism is not an exclusive condition of wealthy, professional people (or any other particular group), but rather a disability that may affect any family. It is also important to keep in mind that most families with a member with autism have other members who are normally developing.

What progress is being made in understanding the causes of autism?

A great deal has yet to be learned about the causes of autism; in fact, experts generally agree that we are in the infancy stage in regard to understanding the disorder. Nonetheless, a number of scientific theories are used to explain autism. In addition, observations and experiments have been used to gain information about the disorder.

Several reasons exist for a lack of clarity regarding the exact cause or causes of autism, including (a) disagreement over the nature and characteristics of autism and pervasive developmental disorders; and (b) the manner in which scientific studies of the cause of human disorders are conducted.

With regard to the nature of autism, children with autism share a number of characteristics with other groups of children with disabilities. For example, some experts may identify a child with intellectual limitations, poor adaptive and social skills, and self-stimulatory behavior as having mental retardation; others may identify the same child as having autism. Still other professionals may use more general terms, such as *developmental disability* or *pervasive developmental disorder,* to describe a child's condition. For youngsters with mild disabilities, professionals may debate whether a child's condition is the result of a learning disability, behavior disorder, or high-functioning autism disorder. Thus, as many parents can attest, autism may be labeled differently by different professionals. This lack of agreement on precisely what constitutes autism makes it difficult to agree on a cause for the syndrome.

To compound matters, autism is a very complex disability, which involves a number of elaborately interrelated and interconnected elements. Thus, children who are identified as having autism may demonstrate different characteristics and levels of functioning. Moreover, children, including those with autism, respond to their world in different ways. This normal complexity of human behavior, in combination with the different symptoms of the disorder, makes it difficult to precisely identify and understand the disability and its causes.

Finally, the manner in which scientific studies are conducted has adversely affected progress in understanding the causes of autism. Scientists who attempt to isolate the cause(s) of autism try to identify factors or conditions that may be associated with the disorder. However, for a number of reasons, it is impossible to fully control and understand these conditions. For example, evidence suggests that autism occurs more frequently among children who develop certain types of medical conditions, such as meningitis. However, every child who is diagnosed as having meningitis does not develop autism; further, scientists do not understand the exact relationship between meningitis and autism. Thus, they may conclude that there is a relationship (referred to as a *correlation*) between autism and certain factors, although this relationship may not be clearly understood to be a cause. This is a fundamental scientific principle and one that must be carefully considered when evaluating any cause-effect relationship. That is, since correlational research is a major means by which scientific knowledge of the causes of disabilities is accumulated, exact reasons for a particular condition are frequently unknown.

What are the different kinds of causes of autism?

Purported causes of autism are divided into two general categories: biological and environmental. *Biological* refers to inborn factors, including medical, physical, biochemical, and genetic conditions. *Environmental* causes (also known as *psychogenic* and *psychological*), on the other hand, refer to conditions and experiences that make up our day-to-day world. Parent, family, school, and community conditions are the environmental influences most frequently mentioned.

Is autism a result of biological influences?

Most current explanations of autism are of a biological nature. In this context, *biological* refers to inborn causal agents, as opposed to environmental factors. Frequently discussed biological factors include genetic influences, neurological abnormalities and impairments, and biochemical abnormalities.

Is autism a genetic disorder?

Genetics refers to heredity. Each time an ovum and sperm unite, they merge into a single cell bearing hereditary characteristics from both parents. Evidence for the significance of genetic influences can be found by observing most families. Body shape, hair color, facial structure, and other physical characteristics link parents to their children and families to their ancestors. Nonphysical characteristics may also be influenced by genetic factors, including temperament and intelligence.

Research indicates that autism may be associated with genetic factors. However, clear support for a genetic link is weak, especially because there does not appear to be a single gene mechanism responsible for autism. That is, although some evidence has shown that genetic influences may play a role in the development of autism, this influence is only a partial explanation. Autism appears to be associated with a variety of genetic mechanisms, thus making the role of heredity in the syndrome difficult to understand. Moreover, genetic influences often interact with environmental factors. That is, a child with autism can be expected to demonstrate certain behavioral patterns; however, family cohesiveness, health, and willingness to accommodate a child with autism significantly affects his or her behavior.

Evidence for a genetic link to autism is in part based on studies of brothers and sisters of children with autism. Findings of these studies reveal that siblings of children with autism are approximately 50 times more apt to be autistic than children in the general population. Studies of twins of children with autism show the chances of both children developing autism as even higher. Studies also reveal that brothers and sisters of autistic children demonstrate a higher incidence of cognitive and language development delays than do children without autistic siblings. Thus, even when brothers and sisters of children with autism are not autistic, they have a higher than average chance of developing cognitive and social problems.

Is autism the result of neurological impairment and/or abnormalities?

Neurological impairment, neurological abnormalities, and *brain damage* are associated with a number of different causes, including oxygen deprivation (e.g., lack of oxygen at birth), disease (e.g., encephalitis), physical trauma (e.g., blow to the head), and congenital malformations (malformations present from birth). Damage to the brain or central nervous system caused by oxygen deprivation, disease, physical trauma, and congenital malformations ranges from severe destruction or malformation of tissue and structures, resulting in death or serious disability, to tiny injuries and malformations that produce little or no behavior change.

Neither the meaning of neurological impairment nor its influence as a cause of autism has been agreed upon. Brain damage suggests dysfunction due to injury or malformation. The damage may be to brain cells (neurons), glia (nonbrain cell materials), blood vessels, or central nervous system structures. If severe, neurological impairment may lead to loss or deterioration of certain functions (e.g., vision, coordination). Damage may occur as a result of lack of oxygen, physical injury, high fever, infection, toxins such as poison or drugs, or brain malformations.

Further, neurological impairment may be permanent or reversible. Neurological impairment is considered to be relatively common, and in most cases is inconsequential. Nearly every child falls and bangs into things, usually with no discernible long-term effect. In one often-quoted medical study of newborn children, examination of spinal fluid one week after birth revealed evidence of blood in half the infants. Blood in this context indicated that some degree of trauma had occurred to the brain or its wrappings in the birth process. However, since most of the infants in the study grew to become healthy children, it is relatively safe to assume that this problem was either minimal or reversible. This conclusion is not intended to minimize the importance of neurological impairment. Although brain damage or neurological malformation can result in serious and permanent disability, most instances of alleged neurological impairment do not entail severe or permanent consequences. Further, there is inconclusive evidence to suggest that such problems are the primary cause of autism.

Hard and *soft* signs are commonly used to describe neurological conditions. A *hard* sign refers to specific neurological damage responsible for a particular problem or deficit. For example, a child with cerebral palsy may experience uncontrolled, jerky, and irregular motor movements. *Soft* damage, on the other hand, refers to an alleged minimal and unidentifiable injury. While the actual damage cannot be identified, it is assumed to exist because of certain behaviors such as hyperactivity or impulsivity.

It is incorrect to conclude that autism is solely the result of neurological impairment; however, at least some individuals with the syndrome give evidence of having some degree of brain or central nervous system dysfunction. The exact nature of these dysfunctions is usually unknown, although brain lateralization dysfunction, malfunctions of brain systems that control arousal, and dysfunction of other brain mechanisms have been implicated.

What is meant by "brain lateralization dysfunction" and how does it relate to autism?

The human brain is composed of two hemispheres, each responsible for certain types of functioning, including specific activities. The dominant hemisphere is thought to be associated with language, while the other controls other functions, such as temporal (relating to time) and spatial relationship activities (relating to space and perception). Increased specialization of the brain occurs with age; however, certain general functions appear to be lateralized in either the right or left hemisphere of the brain from birth. With regard to autism, *brain lateralization dysfunction* refers to the two hemispheres of the brain operating in an atypical fashion. That is, activities and functions usually associated with a particular brain hemisphere occur through activity of the opposite hemisphere. Such "confusion" is thought by some to be at least partially responsible for autism.

What is meant by "brain systems that control arousal" and how are they related to autism?

Using sophisticated medical and behavioral diagnostic procedures, some researchers have concluded that autism may be associated with high levels of arousal. That is, as a result of abnormal brain development, persons with autism may be in a constant high state of stimulation and excitement. Such arousal is thought to interfere with the autistic person's ability to take in and process information and to make appropriate responses.

What is meant by "dysfunction of other brain mechanisms" and how is it related to autism?

According to this explanation of autism, which is based on theory and associated research, components of the brain designed to process sensory information fail to function. As a result, the brain is unable to correctly and meaningfully process sensory information, thus explaining the cognitive, language, and social problems of persons with autism.

What is meant by "biochemical abnormalities" and how are they related to autism?

Our brains consist of masses of cells, called neurons. These nerve cells are designed to receive and transmit information through the use of chemical components called neurotransmitters. Some evidence suggests that failure of these neurotransmitters to function correctly is the basic reason why persons demonstrate characteristics of autism.

One group of neurotransmitters that has received particular notice in studies of autism is monoamines. Monoamines, consisting of serotonin, dopamine, and norepinephrine, are most commonly found in areas of the brain that control emotions and behavior.

Studies have revealed elevated levels of serotonin levels for children and youth with autism. Although serotonin levels vary, some researchers report that the levels for some persons with autism are over 100% of what is considered normal. At present, the relationship between elevated serotonin levels and autistic behaviors and characteristics is unclear. In the absence of precise information, treatment is not clearly defined.

Another neurotransmitter that has been implicated in autism is dopamine, thought to be important in the regulation of motor activities and other functions. It is important to note that dopamine dysfunction in autism has not yet been clearly demonstrated by researchers. Thus, while a few studies have suggested that stereotypic and other behaviors associated with autism can be reduced through use of dopamine reduction, clear evidence is limited.

Epinephrine and norepinephrine disturbances in persons with autism have also been reported. These neurotransmitters play an important role in regulating a number of physiological processes, including breathing, memory, attention, and arousal. However, because of minimal research and inconclusive results, the role of epinephrine and norepinephrine in explaining autism is unknown.

Are there other biochemical explanations for autism?

A number of other biochemical explanations have been proposed, one of them that the brains of persons with autism produce too much of a natural form of opiates, called opioids. Over the past decade, various investigators have theorized that normally developing children, particularly infants, engage in a variety of social behaviors (e.g., seeking their mother's attention), because these activities trigger the brain to release opioids. The brains of children with autism are thought to produce too many opioids, thus explaining their lack of social interest and other abnormal behaviors. There is some research that indicates that administering children with autism medications designed to reduce opioid levels leads to more appropriate behavior, including reductions in self-abuse, self-stimulation, and social withdrawal.

What kinds of conclusions can be drawn about biological causes of autism?

There is no question that certain biological abnormalities are associated with autism. Although none have been delineated as *the cause,* genetic factors, neurological dysfunctions, and biochemical disturbances have all been implicated. The precise role these factors play in explaining autism await further study.

What is meant by "environmental" causes of autism?

Environment is everything external to us. Thus, environmental cause relates to the notion that a child's world, including home experiences, parent and family relationships, community and school experiences, influence his behavior and development. This view is not surprising since it is apparent that the values, attitudes, experiences, and expectations to which children are exposed affect their behavior. Thus, children who are exposed to unhealthy conditions are thought to be more susceptible to a variety of problems.

Are environmental influences the cause of autism?

As mentioned, Leo Kanner, the psychiatrist who originally identified children with autism, concluded that the syndrome, at least in part, originated from a lack of parent affection (e.g., "refrigerator mother"). Others, especially between 1940 and 1969, agreed, supporting the notion that an autistic child's withdrawal and other abnormal responses occurred as a reaction to unfavorable parental personalities (e.g., emotional aloofness) or as a reaction to other adverse environmental conditions (e.g., family stress).

Bruno Bettelheim (1967), a leading proponent of a psychogenic origin of autism, suggested that children with the syndrome perceived their environment as being so cold, threatening, and hostile that they attempted to reject it or shut it out. Thus, autism was seen as an attempt to shut out the world, thereby protecting the child from the perceived hostility.

From the beginning, skeptics have doubted that such conditions, even if present, were the cause of autism. Their resistance was based on several considerations. First, symptoms of autism were often present from birth. Consequently, such extreme reactions as withdrawing from the world would likely not occur as a result of subtle personality characteristics such as emotional distance and aloofness. Furthermore, it was observed that extreme reactions such as totally withdrawing from the world would likely occur only after a while rather than at birth. Finally, it was noted that if psychogenic conditions were responsible for autism, a child's condition would deteriorate over time. However, such deterioration is not common.

Is it correct to conclude that parent and family conditions do not affect children and youth with autism?

The family, typically thought of as consisting of mother, father, and children, has long been considered a primary determinant of a child's personality development and mental health. It is important to recognize, however, that autism is not caused by parents and families. However, this is not to suggest that parents and families do not have a significant influence on children with autism as they do with any child. Thus, parents and families of children and youth with autism have the potential to facilitate development of skills (communication, social, self-help, etc.) as well as behavior and attitudes. Consequently, parents and family members must be viewed as extremely important to the development of children and youth with autism, even though they are not the original cause of the disability.

What sorts of family experiences may affect children and adolescents with autism?

Any one of a number of factors or experiences may influence the behavior and emotional status of children, including those with autism. In particular, conditions that increase parent, family, or children's stress are important, including financial problems, relocation, parent career changes, divorce, role changes (e.g., a mother who takes a job out of the home), and similar situations. Change is not necessarily negative, however. Just because a mother chooses to pursue a career does not mean that a child with autism will suffer. Yet, such changes often increase stress, at least temporarily, especially for children diagnosed as having autism. Since children with autism tend to resist change, shifts in routine, relocation, and similar factors may cause problems (e.g., increase in self-stimulatory behavior, tantrums, sleep disturbances).

An example involves a family, consisting of a mother, a father, and three elementary-age children, one of whom has been diagnosed with autism. As a result of a job opportunity, the family moves from a small town to a large city several hundred miles away. In response to moving from a familiar community, house, neighborhood, babysitter, and grandparents, the child with autism displays a variety of behavior problems, including tantrums, resistance to going to school, and difficulty in completing home tasks he was able to perform prior to the move (e.g., dress himself, verbalize his needs). The child also experiences difficulty at his new school, including an inability to complete tasks he was able to do at his former school and resisting social interactions with his classmates. These problems further increase family stress, already high as a result of adjusting to the move. Thus, the parents and siblings find that they must spend additional time doing things for the child with autism that he was formerly able to do himself (e.g., dress himself); the parents feel compelled to spend a substantial amount of time familiarizing their autistic child's teachers with his background and needs; and the two nonhandicapped siblings report feeling neglected as a result of the parents' increased time investment with the child with autism. These factors increase the family's stress level, which further causes problems in the child with autism. Fortunately, after a few months, the child with autism adapts to his new home and school and the family returns to a more normal existence.

The above example illustrates the potential impact of family experiences on children with autism. Not every child or adolescent with autism will be adversely effected; however, awareness of and sensitivity to the potential of such conditions is important.

What kind of effect does divorce have on children and youth with autism?

The impact of divorce on children and adolescents has been widely debated. While there continues to be more questions than answers some patterns may be discerned. First, children generally seem to respond to the breakup of their families not only in accordance with their unique personalities but also their age and sex. That is, young children respond differently from older children and boys often differently from girls. Further, children usually experience distress over a divorce or separation regardless of the amount of discord and anxiety that existed prior to the separation. That is, contrary to the popular notion that children are relieved after one parent leaves, the opposite often is true. In fact, relief is only common when an abusive parent leaves the home. Further, the relationship that existed between the children and the parent who is leaving is sometimes unrelated to the degree to which children are upset over the breakup of their family. In many cases, children's sadness over a separation or divorce is associated with their grief and anxiety over the breakup of their family rather than how close they were to the departed parent. Children with autism will likely respond to family stress associated with the divorce, parents' reactions to the event, and changes in routine or environment associated with divorce.

In what ways are children with autism affected by their parents' problems following a divorce?

All children and youth can be expected to respond, to varying degrees, to the emotional and personal problems of the adults in their lives.

Three major groups of problems experienced by adults during separation and divorce may affect children and adolescents, including those with autism: financial problems, family management issues, and personal problems.

A major concern of many single parents, especially mothers, is economic survival. According to a number of surveys, the income of families headed by single mothers is less than half that of father-headed homes. Further, over half the children in single-parent homes headed by mothers live below the poverty level. Not only do some mothers find it necessary to seek employment for the first time after divorce, but child support payments from fathers may be irregular or nonexistent. Such economic problems can be expected to reduce the standard of living of many homes, a change that will likely affect children in a family. For example, siblings may be asked to serve as babysitters for their brother or sister with autism, rather than the family being able to hire someone to do the job.

Custodial parents may also experience management problems related to increased responsibility and other changes that typically accompany a divorce. For example, mothers may find that in addition to working full time they are still responsible for all the chores (and maybe more) they handled while they were married. Parents may also find their children more difficult to discipline following a divorce. Some children test their parents after a divorce to see if family rules still exist and if they will be enforced. Just as with nonhandicapped children and adolescents, management concerns may arise with individuals with autism.

Are children and adolescents with autism affected by unhealthy psychological conditions in the home?

Parents' personal problems, especially in combination with an unhealthy home enviroment, may contribute to children's difficulties. Accordingly, unstable and inconsistent parents often have children with behavior problems and skill deficits. This pattern applies to both handicapped and nonhandicapped children. Thus, children with autism generally show the best behavior and social development when their home environments are characterized by structure and consistency. This does not mean that parents *cause* autism; rather, parents have the potential to positively or negatively influence their children's behavior and development, regardless of whether those children are handicapped or normally developing.

One way in which parents may influence children is through their expectations, rules, and management methods. For example, parents who are warm and loving and who clearly and consistently establish expectations, set rules, and follow through with consequences seem to get the best results. While these conditions are extremely important for all children and adolescents, they are mandatory for individuals with autism. That is, under conditions of careful clarification and consistency, children with autism are often able to follow rules, understand expectations, and make the connection between their behavior and the consequences that follow.

Do children and youth with autism respond in the same way in different settings?

The answer to this question is "no." Many autistic children and youth behave differently at home and school. Although they are autistic in both settings, their behavior may be quite different from one setting to another.

Several explanations may be given for such differences. One is related to expectation. That is, children are expected to do different things at school and at home. For example, a child may be motivated and reasonably effective at talking at school because at school he is expected to verbally communicate and reinforced for doing so. However, at home he may be able to communicate and otherwise satisfy his needs without talking (e.g., pointing or crying as a means of getting something).

Another explanation relates to structure. Some children and youth do well at home but not at school because of clearly stated rules and consequences. As noted previously, clarity, consistency, and clearly stated expectations are important for all children and youth; they are mandatory for individuals with autism.

What can schools do to reduce or cause problems of autism?

As is true with parents, schools do not cause autism. However, they can facilitate the growth and development of children and youth with autism in a number of ways.

One obvious way is by providing appropriate educational services. Not all children and youth with autism can be appropriately served in public school settings. Some may be placed in residential and segregated programs for individuals with disabilities. However, the vast majority of children and youth with autism are able to attend public schools when appropriate educational options and support services are available. Not all school districts have specific programs for children and youth with autism; however, since the needs of these students vary significantly, they may be served effectively in a variety of educational settings. Thus, depending on their needs, students with autism may be appropriately assigned to classes for students with mental retardation, learning disabilities, behavior disorders, as well as regular classrooms. Student success in these settings is usually a function of the school's commitment to students with disabilities and availability of appropriate services and resources. Thus, schools must not only offer a variety of effective special education programs, specialists (e.g., language pathologists, occupational and physical therapists, psychologists, curriculum specialists) must also be available who are familiar with programs and methods for children and youth with autism.

Schools systems can significantly contribute to the growth and development of children and youth with autism by providing teachers who are well trained, committed to meeting the needs of every student, and familiar with methods and procedures for students with autism. Even if they do not have a separate program for students with autism, school districts should have educators available who are familiar with methods and procedures for meeting the needs of these students. Teachers of children and youth with autism must also be trained to communicate and cooperate with parents and families. Overwhelming evidence has proven that children and adolescents, including those with autism, make the best progress when parents and educators communicate and work cooperatively.

What can communities do to cause or reduce problems of autism?

Communities are not the cause of autism, however they can support individuals with autism and their families by providing adequate recreational facilities, supportive employment and workshops, vocational programs, independent community living programs, mental health and counseling services, appropriate medical programs, and other support services. Communities can also sponsor programs to increase the public's awareness of the needs of individuals with disabilities, including those with autism. Positive community attitudes towards individuals with disabilities results in a variety of benefits for both disabled and nondisabled persons.

SUMMARY

Autism was initially thought to be caused by parents' personalities, specifically aloofness, psychological coldness, or hostility towards their children. Such interpretations are incorrect. Parents and families are clearly not the cause of autism; however, they can significantly influence their children's growth and development. Most current theories of autism are of a biological or biophysical nature, but no single reason can be pinpointed as *the cause*.

3

Identification and Assessment of Children and Youth with Autism and Pervasive Developmental Disorders

For the reasons discussed earlier, autism is frequently difficult to diagnose, as many parents and families can attest. Many parents and families report that their children are seen by a number of professionals, including psychiatrists, school psychologists, and clinical psychologists, prior to a diagnosis of autism.

Why is it so difficult to make a diagnosis of autism?

Autism is a unique disability; nonetheless, children with autism share characteristics with a number of children with other types of handicaps. As noted in Chapter 1, three primary areas of functioning are considered in making a diagnosis of autism: (a) unresponsive and unusual interactions with people (e.g., withdrawal, lack of eye contact, unwillingness to acknowledge the presence of others); (b) speech and language problems (e.g., delayed speech, echoing others); and (c) unusual behaviors (e.g., self-stimulatory responses, resistance to change). Since these patterns are also shown by children who have disabilities other than autism, it is often difficult for professionals to differentially identify and diagnose children with similar problems. For example, some children with mental retardation have language delays and engage in self-stimulatory behavior. Young children and those with milder forms of autism are particularly difficult to identify.

A second explanation for the identification difficulty derives from the scarcity of tests and procedures specifically designed to diagnose children with autism. Although several tests and diagnostic procedures can be used to assist in identifying children with autism, these scales and methods are not infallible. No test currently available provides conclusive autism results. Moreover, because of the complexity of autism and the many forms it may take, it is unlikely that such an instrument will be developed in the foreseeable future. As a result, professionals must interpret and draw conclusions based on various sources of information (e.g., interviews, observations), often leading to different diagnostic impressions. Differences of professional opinion are particularly evident for children and adolescents with mild symptoms and characteristics of autism.

A final reason why it is difficult to identify children with autism is that parents are often most interested in a diagnosis when their children are very young (i.e., between the ages of 12 and 48 months). Young children, in general, are more difficult to evaluate; besides, tests and procedures designed for children this age are less reliable than those for older children and adolescents.

Why are evaluations conducted if tests and diagnostic procedures do not give precise information about autism?

Evaluations are rarely carried out for the sole purpose of finding out whether or not a child or adolescent has autism. Rather, assessment is designed to provide information about each child or youth's educational, physical, social, and psychological strengths and weaknesses; unique ways of interacting with the world, including people in his home, school and community; and possible problem-solving and treatment options. In fact, evaluations are primarily conducted to develop effective intervention, treatment, and educational programs. For this reason, professionals representing a variety of disciplines (e.g., psychologists, language pathologists, occupational therapists, physicians, educators) should be involved in the evaluation process. On the basis of each child's strengths, weaknesses, and needs, methods and strategies are individualized. Accordingly, an appropriate intervention and educational plan requires accurate and complete assessment information.

Who are the persons who conduct evaluations of children and youth thought to have autism?

Professionals representing a variety of disciplines (specific professions) are involved in an evaluation. These persons may be private practitioners or associated with schools or agencies. The following is a listing of some of these professionals along with a description of their role in the assessment process.

Psychologists.   School and clinical psychologists collect and interpret information about intellectual ability, behavior and personality characteristics, social behaviors, academic achievement level, perceptual and neurological strengths and weaknesses, self-help skills, and language. To gather the necessary data, they use tests, parent and child interviews, and direct observations.

Psychiatrists.   While being concerned with many of the same areas as psychologists, psychiatrists rely more on interviews and direct observations of behavior than tests. In addition, because they hold medical degrees (MD or DO) they may prescribe medications for children, if necessary.

Educators.   Educators test academic strengths and weaknesses and conditions under which learning is best achieved. They are also concerned with children's self-help skills, social interactions, communication abilities, and vocational and prevocational abilities.

Social workers.   Both school and clinical social workers perform a variety of functions. However, their primary job is to serve as a link between evaluation personnel and families, schools, and community agencies. Social workers not only attempt to provide other diagnostic personnel with a complete history of a given child, they also try to obtain relevant information from such sources as physicians and mental health agencies.

Speech pathologists.   Speech pathologists use a variety of tests and procedures to determine the manner in which children receive and process messages and how they communicate. Because children and youth with autism characteristically experience speech and language problems, information gathered by speech and language pathologists is particularly useful.

Audiologists.   These professionals participate in evaluations when a child's ability to hear is questioned. Where indicated, they use various methods and testing procedures to assess children's ability to hear.

Physical therapists.   These professionals use tests as well as their own observational skills to assess physical ability and muscle control. Physical therapists are most likely to participate in evaluations involving neurological or perceptual problems.

Occupational therapists.   Although these staff members appear to be dealing with the same areas as physical therapists, they are more concerned with assessing self-help, daily-living, and similar skills. They use both observational and testing methods.

Medical personnel.   When necessary, medical professionals including nurses, pediatricians, neurologists, family practitioners, and optometrists participate in evaluations. Their specialty skills add to a more thorough understanding of children and youth.

What does an evaluation of a child who is thought to have autism involve?

Children and youth thought to have autism typically demonstrate a number of problems and deficits, including cognitive, language, behavioral, social, medical, educational, and self-help/independent living. Each of these areas requires careful consideration. Accordingly, youngsters' strengths, weaknesses, and needs require a complete and comprehensive evaluation and analysis. *Complete* here means that a variety of individuals representing several professional disciplines (e.g., psychologists, educators, language pathologists) are involved; *comprehensive* refers to the use of an array of procedures and techniques to gain a thorough understanding of a child.

Evaluations may be carried out by either school or clinical professionals. Even though school personnel tend to put more emphasis on educational matters than mental health and other professionals, these groups provide valuable evaluations, making it important for these groups to work together. Such cooperation usually results in more effective understanding and treatment of exceptional children and adolescents, including those with autism. The most important consideration is that the individuals who conduct evaluations are familiar with assessment methods for children with autism.

What areas are considered in evaluations of children and youth with autism?

A variety of methods and procedures are generally used to obtain information in the following areas: cognitive development, environmental conditions, physical/medical, behavioral and social development, speech/language, educational, vocational, and self-help/independent living. Although a number of other areas are also suitable for assessment, these are considered the most relevant.

What is "cognitive development"?

The term *cognitive development* refers to a variety of mental processes, including reasoning, memory, comprehension, and judgment. The term intelligence is sometimes used interchangeably with cognitive ability.

How is cognitive ability measured?

A variety of tests are available for assessing cognitive ability of school age children and youth with average or near-average intellectual ability. These instruments can be divided into two general categories: group and individual scales. For the most part, group tests are pencil-and-paper scales, administered by written or oral directions of a trained examiner to a group of children or adolescents. Typically, these measures are used for large-group assessment, as might be required for induction into the military or admission to a college or university. Although group tests may be used during screening, they are rarely suited for evaluation purposes. Moreover, many children and youth with autism are unable independently to take a group test.

Individualized tests, on the other hand, are designed for use with one person at a time. Administered by a professionally trained examiner, these tests are designed to evaluate cognitive abilities and developmental levels and to allow comparison between individual results and those of a group of persons of similar age and characteristics. The comparison group is referred to as a *standardization sample* or *standardization group*. By means of such standardization groups, a child can be compared to other children of the same age on cognitive abilities, development, and related abilities.

For lower functioning children and youth, fewer options for cognitive assessment are available. Individually administered scales are generally used with children having limited language, limited ability to attend and follow directions, and who may be considered "untestable." These tests generally involve determining (by observation or interview) whether a child or youth has acquired skills typical of children at a certain age (e.g., build a three-block tower, identify body parts, assemble a form-board). Thus, these scales are used to estimate the developmental level of children and adolescents by comparing their performance with that of normally developing children.

How are standardization groups used to judge children's ability and development?

When placed on a graph, cognitive and developmental level test scores produce a bell-shaped curve (Figure 3.1). Imagine, for example, that all students in a school system were given an intelligence test. If their scores were placed on a graph with a baseline ranging from the highest to the lowest IQ scores and another line representing the number of students with a particular score, a large hump would appear in the middle of the curve tapering off at both ends. As shown, this bell-shaped curve simply means that the largest number of intelligence test scores would fall in the middle (average range) of the curve, with high and low scores at the ends. Over half the students would be expected to demonstrate average intellectual ability (IQs between 90 and 110), whereas only about 2% would score in the superior (IQs of 130 and above) or the intellectually deficient range (IQs of 70 and below).

Why is it important to consider cognitive ability?

Children and youth with autism characteristically experience reasoning, comprehension, and judgment deficits. Moreover, they often have difficulty acquiring useful information and skills and may experience developmental delays (e.g., show speech and language delays). Thus, it is important to identify overall cognitive abilities, as well as specific

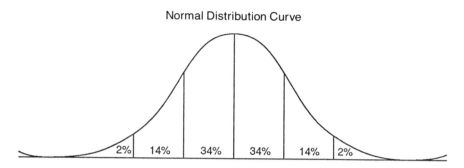

FIGURE 3.1   Percent of cases by portion of normal distribution.

strengths and weaknesses. Further, cognitive ability is considered one of the best predictors of a child's overall prognosis (a prediction of future outcome). While there are exceptions, the cognitive and intellectual abilities of most children and adolescents with autism fall in the retarded range, or on Figure 3.1, in the lower part of the curve.

What tests are used to evaluate cognitive ability?

Children's general abilities and skills determine the types of cognitive and intellectual tests they are given. For example, children and youth possessing spoken language, reasonably good understanding of others' language, and who generally appear to be high functioning (i.e., are developmentally similar to their same age peers) may be given one of three Wechsler intelligence tests.

The *Wechsler Preschool and Primary Scale of Intelligence* (WPPSI) is designed for children between the ages of 4–6; the *Revised Wechsler Intelligence Scale for Children* (WISC-R) is aimed at children and adolescents 6–17, and the *Revised Wechsler Adult Intelligence Scale* (WAIS) at youth 17 and older. Each of these tests yields three separate IQ scores: a verbal IQ, a performance IQ, and a full-scale score (an IQ score based on a combined verbal and performance IQ). As suggested in the name, the verbal scales focus on such areas as vocabulary, fund of general information, and ability to understand social situations. In contrast, the performance areas, which do not require verbal answers, target such skills as forming designs with blocks and putting together puzzle pieces.

Since many children and youth with autism are relatively low functioning (i.e., have limited language, experience difficulty following directions, comprehend poorly), intelligence tests such as the Wechsler series and similar tests designed for their chronological ages are not always appropriate. Thus, it is useless (and professionally unacceptable) to ask a child questions he is unable to understand. Besides yielding little or no useful information, such practices frustrate both children and their families.

An alternative to the more commonly used intelligence tests (e.g., Wechsler scales), useful with lower functioning children and youth, are scales that assess skills associated with particular developmental levels. Often these tests use standardization samples that are younger than the children being assessed. That is, a nonverbal eight-year-old may be evaluated using a developmental scale designed for two- to four-year-olds. Although the eight-year-old cannot be precisely compared with a sample of two- to four-year-olds, a general impression of age equivalents may be obtained. That is, an attempt is made to determine the degree to which the eight-year-old has acquired skills typical of children between the ages of 24 and 48 months. In spite of benefits, most professionals acknowledge that using tests and scales designed for much younger children has limitations.

Cognitive assessment scales used to evaluate lower functioning children include (but are not limited to) the *Bayley Scales of Infant Development, McCarthy Scales of Children's Abilities, Stanford-Binet Intelligence Scale,* and *Leiter International Performance Scale.*

Psychologists and other professionals conducting cognitive evaluations are interested in far more than a child's intelligence. Type and quality of answers as well as behavioral observations, for example, are just as significant for the overall assessment. One psychologist noted that a child asked to duplicate a block pattern using blocks of various colors attended only to the blue blocks. That is, rather than using all available colors to make a design, the child seemed only interested in the blue blocks. Such "stimulus overselectivity" is common among children with autism and was significant for planning the child's educational program.

What is "environmental assessment"?

This type of assessment covers environmental factors that influence behavior. That is, attention has shifted from influences on behavior that are a part of the child (e.g., personality and genetic history) to factors outside the child, such as parents, family, and other environmental conditions. An analysis of these factors provides a better understanding of children and youth and allows professionals to more effectively plan intervention programs.

How is environmental information obtained?

Environmental information is most frequently obtained through a parental (or legal custodian) interview. Because parents have more intimate contact with and possess relevant history about their child, they are the logical source of environmental information. Further, parents tend to be more motivated and have more legal rights to be involved in the evaluation than anybody else. Finally, parents and legal custodians have authority to release to professionals significant records (e.g., medical, educational, psychological), if necessary.

What is involved in a parent interview?

Although each parent interview will have its own emphasis and objectives, certain elements are usually present. Parental impressions are usually sought before parents are given professionals' impressions of their child to avoid influencing their responses. That is, professionals often want descriptions of children's behavior before they relate information about the extent to which a child's behaviors are similar to those of individuals with autism.

Parents should also expect being asked about their child's developmental history. Questions cover significant events, beginning with the parents' histories and continuing to the present. Of primary concern are genetic history; pregnancy or delivery problems; illnesses, accidents, and complications; and the age at which developmental milestones (e.g., walking, toilet training, and speech) were achieved. Much of this information may be obtained prior to the interview from previous records and from asking parents to complete a developmental history form.

Another frequent subject of parent interviews is parents' perception of their child's personality and his or her behavior and attitude toward friends, family, school, and so forth. Interviewers are also interested in parents' description of their child's likes and dislikes, characteristics, and leisure activities. In addition, parents may be asked about their children's patterns of aggression, withdrawn behavior, and other similar responses.

For school-age children, a child's educational history according to the parents' perception constitutes a part of the interview. In this connection, parents are usually asked to describe their child's school-related history (e.g., schools attended), as well as previous professional measures taken to diagnose or remediate home or school difficulties.

Parents' expectations for their children also play a part in the interview. In particular, the interviewer is interested in goals parents and family members have for youngsters, and whether these goals match their abilities and skills.

Finally, interviewers will attempt to obtain information to aid them in better understanding a child's environment. This includes the family membership and its cultural and ethnic makeup; the economic standing of the family, including the parents' occupation; the mental and physical health of family members; languages other than English spoken by the parents or others in the family; parental child-rearing practices; and amount of supervision and contact children receive.

Again, the intent of the parent interview is to provide evaluators with a better understanding of a child's world and background. Such understanding facilitates understanding of and sensitivity to children and the development of effective intervention and training programs.

Why is it important to consider physical and medical factors during evaluations?

The relationship between autism and medical and physical factors has been well documented. For example, conditions such as maternal rebulla, meningitis, encephalitis, and tubular sclerosis have been associated with autism. Moreover, it is not unusual for parents of children with autism to have physical and medical concerns about their child (e.g., ability to hear, sleeping disturbances, eating problems). Thus, accurate diagnoses and subsequent treatment and intervention with children and youth with autism is enhanced by medical and physical information. In addition, many children with autism may be considered for drug treatment at some point, thus necessitating availability of relevant medical information.

How is physical and medical information obtained?

Most physical/medical information is based on observations (e.g., examination by a physician), medical tests (e.g., seizure disorder evaluations) or tests designed to assess areas other than physical functioning (e.g., evidence of possible hearing impairment during cognitive testing).

The specific nature of examinations by a psychiatrist, neurologist, pediatrician, or other physician of children thought to have autism will vary in accordance with children's symptoms, abilities, and age. For instance, a child who has seizures will likely be examined specifically with reference to his neurological problems; children who are cooperative and verbal are dealt with differently than nonverbal, noncompliant children; finally, children's ages influence how examinations and evaluations are structured.

Most physicians who examine children thought to have autism are concerned about their pattern of growth and development. Specifically, they will focus on children's physical, language, mental, and emotional development, with reference to how they compare to normally developing children.

Most physicians, including psychiatrists and neurologists, are also interested in the child's and family's medical history, including parents' concerns about their children (including illnesses, complaints, and problems), emotional, physical, environmental and social histories, and current conditions of children and their families. Questions may include: Was the child separated from his parents for an extended period at an early age? Did child and mother receive prenatal care? Were there birth complications? What was the mother's physical and mental health while she was pregnant with the child? Did the child suffer an injury at an early age? What childhood diseases and illness did the child have? What is the emotional climate of the home?

Physicians will also typically observe children and youth. Thus, they will examine children's manner and appearance; awareness of surroundings, people, places, and time; capacity to respond to directives; mood, affect, and emotional responses; activity level, response to external stimuli, and self-stimulatory behaviors; perceptual accuracy (i.e., does the child see and hear what others are seeing and hearing); memory and cognitive abilities; speech and language; judgment (i.e., capacity to behave appropriately and make decisions); and interactions with others.

Finally, physicians will frequently conduct a physical examination of the child, similar to what any child goes through when they visit a physician (e.g., temperature, blood pressure, investigation of physical abnormalities, systems review). Moreover, children suspected of having autism are often evaluated for neurological problems. Specifically, the following is frequently assessed: cranial nerve functioning (12 nerves that run from the brain stem and control various bodily functions), sight, smell, symmetry (balance of child across the parts of his body), balance, coordination, sensory sensitivity (e.g., response to light and deep touch), deep tendon reflexes (e.g., child's response to having his knee tapped), hand and foot dominance, and ability to engage in various motor activities (e.g., skip, catch a ball). If indications of abnormality are detected, specific tests will be requested. For instance, a doctor may request an EEG (electroencephalogram, an examination of the electrical activity of the brain) if neurological abnormality is suspected.

How is physical and medical information used in evaluations?

Physical and medical information is often of greatest value when interpreted along with other diagnostic information. This was found to be the case in the evaluation of a 3-year-old boy. During the assessment his mother reported that he frequently "would stare off into space," during which time he "went blank." Investigation of this pattern by a neurologist revealed that the child was having seizures. While drug treatment of the seizure disorder did not "cure" the boy's autism, he was better able to benefit more from educational and behavioral interventions subsequent to medical assistance.

How is behavioral and social development evaluated?

The nature of behavioral and social evaluations varies depending on the person conducting them as well as the children and adolescents under study. In general, however, psychologists, educators, psychiatrists and other professionals (e.g., language pathologists, occupational therapists) use three basic methods: (a) observations, (b) tests and rating scales, and (c) interviews.

How are observations used in behavioral and social evaluations?

Behavioral observation methods, the most direct form of behavioral and social evaluation, make no assumptions about the meaning of responses to artificial situations. That is, rather than attempting to determine if a child is socially withdrawn based on how he describes a picture or an ink blot (something many children with autism are unable to do), the child's interactions with others are directly observed.

This approach is based on the assumption that the best way to understand children's social and behavioral strengths and weaknesses is to directly observe them. Children are not only observed in clinical settings (e.g., professionals' offices), but in other significant environments as well, including home and school.

An example of a direct observation procedure, designed for children and youth undergoing evaluations for autism, is shown in Figure 3.2. Developed by Simpson and Regan (1986), the system allows for observations in six major areas: (a) stereotypic/self-stimulatory behaviors, (b) aggressive behavior, (c) speech and language, (d) self-help/independent living skills, (e) social skills, and (f) independent work habits. Using the *Informal Observation Data Sheet* (Figure 3.2), trained observers record a definition of a behavioral target (e.g., self-stimulatory rocking); how frequently the behavior occurs (e.g., number of rocks within a 30-minute period); duration of the target behavior (e.g., length of time rocking occurs within a 30-minute period); where the target behavior occurs (e.g., child primarily rocks at home); and other descriptive information (e.g., child will stop rocking for short periods of time with reminder).

The most effective way of understanding children and adolescents is to watch what they do in those settings where they experience problems. Thus, a child who engages in self-stimulatory hand flapping at school is best understood through direct observation at school.

What are rating scales and how are they used?

This form of assessment tool requires that someone familiar with a child or adolescent (e.g., a parent or teacher) evaluate their behavior using a structured form. Specifically, persons completing the forms are asked to rate children's behavior. Ratings may take the form of "yes" or "no" responses or evaluations on particular dimensions (e.g., Does child prefer to be alone? never . . . occasionally . . . often . . . a great deal).

An example of a behavior rating scale, shown in Figure 3.3, is the *Behavior Checklist*, developed by Simpson and Regan (1986). This rating scale allows information to be gathered in several significant areas (e.g., communication, social skills) from several sources, including teachers, parents, and family members.

Another example of rating scale items is shown in Figure 3.4. Drawn from the behavioral rating scale part of the *Autism Screening Instrument for Educational Planning* (Krug, Arick, & Almond, 1980), this popular evaluation tool allows professionals to compare children and youth with autism with other groups of disabled and nondisabled children.

Behavioral ratings are used for evaluative purposes as well as treatment planning. That is, in addition to providing a method for evaluating a child or youth's social and behavioral development, these measures can

Name:_____ Date:_____ Observer:_____

Time of observation: _____ to: _____

Description of observation environment: _____

_____

Behavior	Specific description	Frequency of occurrence	Duration of occurrence	Site of occurrence	Comments
Example: Light filtering	Holds hands slightly higher than eye level; moves fingers back and forth. Fixed stare on finger movements.	ᴺᴺ ᴺᴺ ᛁ	30–50 sec.	Free time at desk	
I. Stereotypic/Self-Stimulatory Behaviors					
Light filtering					
Arm waving					
Object waving (paper, pencil)					
Object waving (twirling)					
Hand wringing					
Tapping (object or self)					
Smelling objects					
Body contortions/bizarre torso extensions					
Spinning self or objects					
Rocking					
Drooling/ playing with saliva					

Behavior	Specific description	Frequency of occurrence	Duration of occurrence	Site of occurrence	Comments
Walking on toes					
Tooth flicking					
Grinding teeth					
Thumb-sucking					
Mouthing objects					
Ear plugging					
Covering eyes					
Banging hands to-gether on a metal surface					
Other noisemaking					
Ruminating					

II. Aggressive Behaviors

Throwing					
Hitting self/others					
Grabbing objects or hitting with objects					
Biting self/others					
Hair pulling					
Tearing or shredding objects					

FIGURE 3.2 Continued.

Behavior	Specific description	Frequency of occurrence	Duration of occurrence	Site of occurrence	Comments
Tantrumming- (crying, screaming, hitting, biting)					
Head banging					

III. Speech/Language Behaviors

Echolalic speech					
Inappropriate vocalizations (nonsense words, jargon, phrases					
Self- stimulatory vocalizations					
Self-talking					
Inappropriate laughing/ giggling					
Unrespon- siveness to speech of others					
Nonverbal responses to commands/ questions					

IV. Self-Care/Independent Living Skills

Behavior	Specific description	Frequency of occurrence	Duration of occurrence	Site of occurrence	Comments
Toilet training					
Self-feeding					
Self-grooming (brushing teeth, combing hair, washing face and hands)					
Self-dressing					

V. Social Skills

Behavior	Specific description	Frequency of occurrence	Duration of occurrence	Site of occurrence	Comments
Noncompliance					
Lack of response to adults/peers					
Fearful					
Lack of eye contact					
Negative response to touch of adults/peers					
Isolates self					
Lack awareness of adults/peers					

FIGURE 3.2   Continued.

VI. Independent Work Habits

Behavior	Specific description	Frequency of occurrence	Duration of occurrence	Site of occurrence	Comments
Stays on task					
Stays in seat					
Works in-dependently without reinforcement					
Moves from activity to ac-tivity on request					
Follows 1-2-3-step directions					

Note preferences (toys, edibles, objects in room, etc.) which might serve as reinforcers:

FIGURE 3.2 Informal observation data sheet. *Note.* From *Management of Autistic Behavior* (pp. 4:16–4:20) by Richard L. Simpson and Madelyn Regan, 1986, Austin: TX: PRO-ED. Copyright 1986 by PRO-ED. Reprinted by permission.

also direct the focus of treatment. For example, if a child is consistently perceived as having poor social interaction skills, this problem can be made a part of the treatment.

How is interviewing used in behavioral and social evaluations?

The nature and content of interviews vary depending on the person being interviewed (e.g., child, parent, teacher). Children or youth with good language and cognitive abilities may be interviewed. Such interviews will focus on many of the same areas as the parent interview. For instance, children and adolescents may be asked to describe their problems along with the causes of the reported difficulties. Youngsters may also be encouraged to discuss their personality traits, attitude toward home, school, friends, family, leisure-time activities, as well as likes and dislikes. Special attention will probably be paid to descriptions of their relationships with family and peers. Finally, youngsters may be encouraged to describe their home and family life.

Many children and youth being evaluated for autism are unable to respond to interview questions. Thus, others, including parents, family members, and teachers, may be interviewed instead. In addition to questions asked of parents (see section in this chapter entitled "What's involved in a parent interview?"), teachers may be asked to provide information. An example of such information, shown in Figure 3.5, is that sought via a teacher interview format developed by Simpson and Regan (1986).

Interview content also varies depending on the person conducting the interview and the age and problems of the child under study. For instance, psychiatrists will likely be more interested in medically related information than psychologists, whereas educators will probably be most interested in children's school experiences and learning potential. Similarly, interviews of persons connected with school-age children will focus, in part, on educational and school-related matters, whereas interviews of preschool children will address home and community issues.

Why is it important to consider speech and language abilities as a part of an evaluation?

As noted, communication problems represent a significant disturbance of children and youth with autism. Virtually all children and adolescents with autism have speech and language problems. As mentioned in Chapter 1, speech refers to forming and using the sounds of oral language, while language is a broader term referring to use of a communication system. Speech problems may take the form of making and using incorrect speech sounds, while language problems may be an inability to effectively communicate with others.

Children's speech and language development is so important and integral to other areas of development (e.g., cognitive development, social interactions) that professionals give it particular attention during evaluations. The importance of children and youth with autism developing an effective communication system explains this emphasis.

How is speech and language functioning evaluated?

A variety of techniques exist for evaluating children's communication systems, including tests, interviews, observations, and clinical methods

Student: Teacher: Date:

Instructions: Circle a response in the left-hand column for each item that describes the student: N—Never, S—Sometimes, O—Often, No—No opportunity to observe.

Communication

N	S	O	NO	1. Indicates needs by gestures.
N	S	O	NO	2. Makes inappropriate verbalizations. Specify:
N	S	O	NO	3. Is echolalic; repeats sounds, words, or phrases.
N	S	O	NO	4. Whispers instead of talking.
N	S	O	NO	5. Speech appears uncommunicative.
N	S	O	NO	6. Substitutes nouns and pronouns for "I" statements.
N	S	O	NO	7. Substitutes words for other words.
N	S	O	NO	8. Speech appears unrelated to actions.
N	S	O	NO	9. Acts as if deaf.
N	S	O	NO	10. Does not answer others' questions.
N	S	O	NO	11. Uses little inflection or expression in voice.
N	S	O	NO	12. Appears not to understand others' speech.
N	S	O	NO	13. Uses questions or phrases for "no."
N	S	O	NO	14. Avoids using pronouns in speech.
N	S	O	NO	15. Repeats questions.
N	S	O	NO	16. Reverses pronouns in speech.
N	S	O	NO	17. Uses prepositions and pronouns as nouns.
N	S	O	NO	18. Verbally fixates on specific objects, characters, or events. Specify:
N	S	O	NO	19. Uses baby talk and/or paints instead of using appropriate language. Clarification:

Learning

Patterns

N	S	O	NO	20. Resists learning situations.
N	S	O	NO	21. Appears oblivious to real dangers.
N	S	O	NO	22. Demonstrates a good verbal memory for words repeated often.
N	S	O	NO	23. Appears preoccupied with isolated sensory input; cannot ignore extraneous stimuli.
N	S	O	NO	24. Demonstrates "splinter skills" (unusually high-level skills incongruous with functioning pattern).
N	S	O	NO	25. Learns a simple task but "forgets" easily.
N	S	O	NO	26. Has difficulty following teacher directions.
N	S	O	NO	27. Uses poor visual discrimination when learning (tends to fixate on single characteristics). Clarification:

Functional Skills

N	S	O	NO	28. Has difficulty running simple errands. Clarification:
N	S	O	NO	29. Avoids asking for needed help. Clarification:
N	S	O	NO	30. Has difficulty feeding self. Clarification:
N	S	O	NO	31. Has difficulty dressing self. Clarification:
N	S	O	NO	32. Has difficulty taking care of personal grooming. Clarification:
N	S	O	NO	33. Fails to identify self by name. Clarification:
N	S	O	NO	34. Has difficulty taking care of toileting needs. Clarification:

Social Relatedness

Personal Characteristics

N	S	O	NO	35. Laughs inappropriately.
N	S	O	NO	36. Demonstrates inappropriate attachments to objects.

N	S	O	NO	37. Spins objects.
N	S	O	NO	38. Demonstrates sustained odd play.
N	S	O	NO	39. Demonstrates marked physical overactivity.
N	S	O	NO	40. Engages in self-destructive behavior.
N	S	O	NO	41. Makes poor use of leisure time.
N	S	O	NO	42. Appears happiest when left alone.
N	S	O	NO	43. Smiles inappropriately.
N	S	O	NO	44. Grimaces or conceals eyes in natural light.
N	S	O	NO	45. Feels, smells, and/or tastes objects in the environment.
N	S	O	NO	46. Engages in ritualistic behavior, such as ordering objects.
N	S	O	NO	47. Shows difficulty caring for personal belongings.
N	S	O	NO	48. Has hypochondrical tendencies.
N	S	O	NO	49. Frustrates easily when challenged.
N	S	O	NO	50. Stares into space.
N	S	O	NO	51. Engages in rhythmical movements of the body (i.e., rocks).
N	S	O	NO	52. Repeats play patterns mechanically.
N	S	O	NO	53. Twists.
N	S	O	NO	54. Makes facial grimaces.
N	S	O	NO	55. Spins self.
N	S	O	NO	56. Jumps.
N	S	O	NO	57. Flaps hands, arms.
N	S	O	NO	58. Walks on toes.
N	S	O	NO	59. Bangs or twirls objects.
N	S	O	NO	60. Is destructive with own property.
N	S	O	NO	61. Appears sluggish and lethargic.
N	S	O	NO	62. Swears.
N	S	O	NO	63. Appears nervous and jittery; is easily startled.

Reaction to Others

N	S	O	NO	64. Cries easily.
N	S	O	NO	65. Has temper tantrums.
				Clarification:
N	S	O	NO	66. Fights with peers.
N	S	O	NO	67. Is easily led by others.
N	S	O	NO	68. Is destructive with others' property.
N	S	O	NO	69. Avoids activity with others.
N	S	O	NO	70. Fails to show consideration for others.
N	S	O	NO	71. Takes others' property without permission.
N	S	O	NO	72. Appears disinterested in strangers.
N	S	O	NO	73. "Looks or walks through" people.
N	S	O	NO	74. Is standoffish toward familiar people.
N	S	O	NO	75. Establishes little eye contact.
N	S	O	NO	76. Resists physical affection.
N	S	O	NO	77. Has difficulty mixing with other children.
N	S	O	NO	78. Behaves passively toward others.
				Clarification:

Reaction to Authority

N	S	O	NO	79. Resists change in routine.
N	S	O	NO	80. Attends poorly in group situations.
N	S	O	NO	81. Reacts poorly to criticism.
N	S	O	NO	82 Demonstrates disruptive or resistive behavior.
N	S	O	NO	83. Talks back.
N	S	O	NO	84. Displays negativism; tends to do the opposite of what is requested.
N	S	O	NO	85. Is easily embarrassed.
N	S	O	NO	86. Attends poorly in 1-to-1 situations.
				Clarification:

This checklist was based on information presented in DeMyer, Churchill, Pontius, & Gilkey (1971); Nihira, Foster, Shellhaas, & Leland (1975); and Rendle-Short (1978).

FIGURE 3.3 Autism behavior checklist. *Note.* From *Management of Autistic Behavior* (pp. 4:4–4:5) by Richard L. Simpson and Madelyn Regan, 1986, Austin, TX: PRO-ED. Copyright 1986 by PRO-ED. Reprinted by permission.

AUTISM BEHAVIOR CHECKLIST

Student's Name _____

Date _____

Examiner _____

INSTRUCTIONS: Circle the number to indicate the items that most accurately describe the child.

	Sensory	Relating	Body and Object Use	Language	Social and Self-Help
	1	2	3	4	5
Whirls self for long periods of time			4		
Learns a simple task but "forgets" quickly					2
Child frequently does not attend to social/environmental stimuli		4			
Does not follow simple commands which are given once (sit down, come here, stand up)				1	
Does not use toys appropriately (spins tires, etc.)			2		
Poor use of visual discrimination when learning (fixates on one characteristic such as size, color or position)	2				
Has no social smile		2			
Has pronoun reversal (you for I, etc.)				3	
Insists on keeping certain objects with him/her			3		
Seems not to hear, so that a hearing loss is suspected	3				
Speech is atonal and arhythmic				4	
Rocks self for long periods of time			4		
Does not (or did not as a baby) reach out when reached for		2			
Strong reactions to changes in routine/environment					3
Does not respond to own name when called out among two others (Joe, **Bill**, Mary)				2	
Does a lot of lunging and darting about, interrupting with spinning, toe walking, flapping, etc.			4		
Not responsive to other people's facial expressions/feelings		3			
Seldom use "yes" or "I"				2	
Has "special abilities" in one area of development, which seems to rule out mental retardation					4
Does not follow simple commands involving prepositions ("put the ball on the box" or "put the ball in the box")				1	
Sometimes shows no "startle response" to a loud noise (may have thought child was deaf)	3				
Flaps hands				4	
Severe temper tantrums and/or frequent minor tantrums					3
Actively avoids eye contact		4			
Resists being touched or held		4			
Sometimes painful stimuli such as bruises, cuts and injections evoke no reaction	3				
Is (or was as a baby) stiff and hard to hold		3			
Is flaccid (doesn't cling) when held in arms		2			
Gets desired objects by gesturing				2	
Walks on toes			2		
Hurts others by biting, hitting, kicking, etc.					2
Repeats phrases over and over				3	
Does not imitate other children at play			3		
Often will not blink when a bright light is directed toward eyes	1				
Hurts self by banging head, biting hand, etc.			2		
Does not wait for needs to be met (wants things immediately)					2
Cannot point to more than five named objects				1	
Has not developed any friendships		4			
Covers ears at many sounds	4				
Twirls, spins and bangs objects a lot			4		
Difficulties with toilet training					1
Uses 0-5 spontaneous words per day to communicate wants and needs				2	
Often frightened or very anxious		3			
Squints, frowns or covers eyes when in the presence of natural light	3				
Does not dress self without frequent help					1
Repeats sounds or words over and over				3	
"Looks through" people		4			
Echoes questions or statements made by others				4	
Frequently unaware of surroundings, and may be oblivious to dangerous situations					2
Prefers to manipulate and be occupied with inanimate things					4
Will feel, smell and/or taste objects in the environment			3		
Frequently has no visual reaction to a "new" person	3				
Gets involved in complicated "rituals" such as lining things up, etc.			4		
Is very destructive (toys and household items are soon broken)			2		
A developmental delay was identified at or before 30 months of age					1
Uses at least 15 but less than 30 spontaneous phrases daily to communicate				3	
Stares into space for long periods of time	4				
TOTALS					
	1 +	2 +	3 +	4 +	5 =

FIGURE 3.4 Autism behavior checklist. *Note.* From *Autism Screening Instrument for Education Planning* (ASIEP) (Scoring and Record Form) by David A. Krug, Joel R. Arick, and Patricia J. Almond, 1980, Austin, TX: PRO-ED. Copyright 1980 by PRO-ED. Reprinted by permission.

(specific procedures used by speech pathologists and other communication experts). More and more, experts rely on procedures that allow them to understand communication systems within the context of children's individual worlds. Thus, professionals want to understand how children communicate their needs at home and in other natural settings; how they relate their feelings and concerns; and how they interact with people. For instance, does a child lead his mother to the sink to let her know he wants a drink of water? Does he run around when he needs to use a toilet? Does he cry in response to a disruption in household routine? Information of this type is most useful in the development of intervention programs.

Speech and language assessment typically is not designed to compare children's nonfunctional communication abilities (i.e., those infrequently used in day-to-day interactions) with those of their same-age peers, but to discover a child's communication strengths and weaknesses along with strategies for improving communication. For example, it may be of little value to confirm through test results that a child knows the meaning of fewer words than his same-age peers. Instead, professionals involved in speech and language evaluations are most interested in knowing about the communication methods used by children and youth in their day-to-day interactions as well as methods for improving these skills.

Speech and language assessment may take a variety of forms: parents, family members, and teachers may be interviewed; children and youth may be observed in a variety of natural settings (e.g., classroom, home, babysitter's house); and children may be engaged in functional tasks designed to uncover their communication strengths, weaknesses, and strategies. Each of these approaches yields unique information; thus, each is needed to understand children's communication. Furthermore, only a multifaceted approach can yield the information needed to identify strategies for improving children's speech and language systems.

Why is it important to consider academic abilities as a part of assessment?

Virtually all children and youth with autism will demonstrate academic achievement problems. However, not all children and youth with autism will be working in an "academic curriculum." For instance, it is unlikely that a 17-year-old with poor communication skills, mental retardation, and severe behavior problems is able to read and do mathematics. At the same time, it is unlikely that reading and writing are emphasized in his curriculum, given his other needs and his limited potential for

Interviewer: _____   Date: _____
Informant: _____
Student: _____   Sex: M   F   Race: _____
Date of birth: _____   Grade: _____
Home address/phone: _____
Teacher statement of student problem: _____
_____
_____

EDUCATIONAL SETTING

1. No. of students in class: boys: _____   girls: _____
2. No. of full-time teachers: _____   aides: _____
3. Description of class (regular vs. special, traditional vs. open concept): _____
_____
4. Description of teaching style (structured vs. unstructured): _____
_____
5. Description of class seating arrangement(s) (including rows, clusters, isolation booths): _____
_____
6. Special seating for student (including proximity to board or teacher; isolation; other): _____
_____
7. Important physical features of the class: _____
8. Additional information: _____
_____

PARENT COMMUNICATION

1. No. of parent conferences this year: _____   attending parent(s): _____
2. Special parent communication systems in operation (including a description of type of frequency): _____
_____
   parent role/followthrough in communication systems: _____
_____
3. Other specialists/agencies involved: _____
4. Description of teacher relationship with parents (including parent attitude toward school/cooperation): _____
_____
5. Additional information: _____
_____

HEALTH/PHYSICAL CONSIDERATIONS

1. Current medications: _____
2. Allergies: _____
3. Seizures or convulsions: _____
4. Vision: _____
5. Hearing: _____
6. Speech problems: _____
7. Motor skills: fine: _____   gross: _____
8. Other health/physical problems: _____
9. Classroom or teaching modifications as a result of health/physical considerations (including special PE, motor programming, limited recess, modified behavior programs): _____
_____
10. Additional information: _____
_____

ACADEMIC FUNCTIONING

1. Academic strengths: _____
   weaknesses: _____
2. Academic likes: _____
   dislikes: _____

3. Test data:
   IQ _____   Source(s) _____
   Reading _____   Source(s) _____
   Math _____   Source(s) _____
   Spelling _____   Source(s) _____
   Language arts _____   Source(s) _____
   Speech _____   Source(s) _____
   Other _____   Source(s) _____
4. Performance levels:
   Reading _____
   Math _____
   Spelling _____
   Language arts _____
   Speech _____
   Other _____
5. Spec. ed. services received: _____
6. Rate of learning (including progress on academic goals): _____
   _____
7. Impression(s) of school attitude: _____
8. Additional information: _____
   _____
   _____
   _____

PERSONAL AND SOCIAL ADJUSTMENT

1. Behavior Checklist: complete form (Exhibit 4-2).
2. Management techniques: _____
   _____
   _____
3. Reinforcers/likes (identify spontaneous vs. elicited) (refer to Checklist of School Reinforcers): _____
   _____
4. Punishers/dislikes (identify spontaneous vs. elicited) (refer to Checklist of School Reinforcers): _____
   _____
5. Leisure-time activities: _____
6. Other special problems or situations (including reactions to lunch, field trips, specials, substitutes): _____
   _____
7. Additional information: _____
   _____

IMPRESSIONS

(Include a statement of teacher and student needs and goals, responses or comments from other school personnel concerning the student, overall teacher impressions of the student, special parent considerations or areas to probe.)

FIGURE 3.5   Teacher interview form. *Note.* From *Management of Autistic Behavior* (pp. 4:7–4:8) by Richard L. Simpson and Madelyn Regan, 1986, Austin, TX: PRO-ED. Copyright 1986 by PRO-ED. Reprinted by permission.

academic success. For this student, therefore, it would be more typical that a curriculum emphasizing social skill development, communication, vocational training, independent living and other basic skills would precede academic training.

Many children and youth with autism will have the potential to pursue an academic curriculum, at least in part. Thus, knowledge of these children's academic strengths and weaknesses must be identified and understood so that suitable programs can be planned. Assessment of academic skills and abilities, therefore, must be a part of the overall evaluation.

Do other evaluation areas receive consideration?

"Yes." In addition to cognitive development, environment, physical/ medical status, behavior/social development, speech/language, and educational strengths and weaknesses, assessment of children and youth for autism and pervasive developmental disorders may include consideration of vocational skills and aptitude for independent living. These areas are particularly significant for youth and young adults, but may also be evaluated in children.

What does a vocational evaluation involve?

Except in instances where youth are being considered for placement in a workshop setting or other job role, evaluations do not ordinarily provide in-depth analysis of children and adolescents' vocational skills. However, an attempt is often made to provide a general impression of an individual's readiness for a work or vocational setting. For example, task compliance, ability to work without direct supervision, social interaction skills, and other factors and behaviors deemed significant in successfully placing persons with autism in work and vocational settings may be considered. The vocational area is considered significant because many individuals with autism will be placed in workshop, supported employment, and similar settings as adults. While demands for workshop and other types of vocational programs for adults with autism far outweigh the availability of such services, educational programs must nonetheless provide appropriate diagnostic and training programs so that children and youth may compete for available workshop positions.

What does an evaluation of independent living potential involve?

This part of an assessment is designed to determine the extent to which an individual is able to live independently or semi-independently, and what types of training he or she will need to become more independent. For instance, can an individual take care of self-care needs (e.g., grooming, shaving)? Select and prepare food? Use public transportation? Use money? Engage in appropriate leisure-time activities? This component is particularly significant when an adolescent or young adult is being assessed. However, independent living skills are so important that they are also considered in evaluations of children.

Few tests adequately evaluate independent living skills. As a result, information in this area is usually obtained through interviews with parents and family members and direct observations. While useful in making diagnoses of autism, independent living information is most helpful in selecting training goals. Thus, for example, a child who is unable to brush his teeth would likely be scheduled to learn this skill.

Are evaluations of children and adolescents thought to have autism always the same?

"No." Since children and youth are unique, evaluations must be specifically designed. Therefore, beyond evaluations in the previously discussed general areas (i.e., cognitive development, environmental conditions, physical/medical, behavioral/social development, speech/language, and educational), specific procedures are used to answer individual questions. For example, a portion of the speech and language evaluation of a nonverbal child with a cleft palate (an opening in the roof of the mouth) would likely focus on determining the extent to which the child's communication problems are attributable to his physical impairment. Thus, the procedures used with this child would be different from those used with a child whose physical development was normal.

How do I get my child evaluated?

Evaluations can be obtained from professionals in private clinical settings; city, county, state, and other public facilities; and school districts. Individuals seeking an evaluation of a child manifesting characteristics of autism should contact their private physican or local, county, or state medical society (or a university medical center); local, county, or state mental-health association; director of special education of their local school district; or the local, state, or national Autism Society of America (ASA; see Appendix for address of ASA national office) for referral information. Early intervention is a key to effective intervention with children with autism. Therefore, parents suspecting a problem should not wait for the situation to improve on its own—it usually will not happen. Additional details on seeking an evaluation are provided in Chapter 8.

SUMMARY

Assessment represents a significant part of meeting the needs of children and youth with autism and pervasive developmental disorders. Even though autism is often difficult to diagnose, special procedures are available for this purpose. With skillful application of these methods, children and youth requiring professional attention can be identified and receive appropriate training, education, and treatment.

4

Major Problems and Needs of Children and Youth with Autism

In this chapter we will take a closer look at the problems exhibited by children and youth with autism and pervasive developmental disorders. Autism and similar developmental disorders are not subtle. Thus, children and youth diagnosed as such are obvious to most observers. Their behaviors, whether extremely disturbing to others or extremely withdrawn, usually draw significant attention. Except for persons with higher functioning autism disorders, these behaviors are so severe that many of these individuals will not live totally independent lives.

It is extremely difficult to pinpoint particular *types* of individuals as having autism. Children with severe autism are usually identified within the first three years of life. However, some children identified as autistic may have their diagnosis changed later on. Further, many experts believe that the label "autism" is insufficient for understanding the condition and that, consequently, additional descriptors are needed.

As mentioned, much time and effort have been devoted to identifying and assessing children and youth with autism. Throughout this process, the ultimate purpose should be remediation, based on the belief that if characteristics can be identified and perhaps categorized, a better understanding and treatment will result. However, although many of the characteristics of autism are agreed upon, others are surrounded by confusion. Thus, many of the characteristics that will be discussed in this chapter are also evident in persons with mental retardation and other disabilities population.

Further, the nature of autism makes it very difficult to obtain accurate intelligence measurements. For example, according to one study, about 80% of persons with autism may have intelligence quotients (IQs) in the retarded range, similar to individuals who have been diagnosed as mentally retarded. And, yet, some autistic children and youth have exceptional memories, motor skills, and so forth.

In this chatper, we have divided the problems associated with autism into broad categories (a) developmental, (b) sensory, (c) social, (d) speech and language, and (e) unique abilities. Yet, problems within one of these categories may interact with those of another. For example, a child with language and speech problems may also experience social problems because of an inability to communicate verbally.

CAUTION: The behaviors identified below may only be indicative of autism when intensity, pattern, and duration are considered (see Chapter 1). Certainly, most human beings exhibit these behaviors in less exaggerated instances from time to time.

DEVELOPMENTAL RATE AND SEQUENCE PROBLEMS

As mentioned in Chapter 1, many children and youth with autism demonstrate developmental delays in three general areas: cognition, social adaptation, and motor. Cognition and social-adaptation delays are universal; motor problems are common within this population. Before we can discuss the delay notion, however, it is necessary to understand "normal" cognitive, social/adaptive, and motor development.

Defining normality is not easy. Statistically, behaviors can be measured and identified with certain age groups. Thus, four- and five-year-olds exhibit certain behaviors that have not yet developed in "normal" two- or three-year-olds. Accordingly, if an eight-year-old child cannot perform tasks normally mastered by a three- or four-year-old, there is cause for concern.

Often cognition is the easiest developmental delay to identify. A cognitive developmental delay is commonly labeled as mental retardation. For example, an eight-year-old child has the intellectual capability of a four-year-old. Some skills (such as toileting, talking) may be delayed, appear and then disappear, or never appear at all. There is little direct evidence to suggest that a cognitive developmental delay of an individual with autism is the same as "mental retardation."

Much controversy surrounds the "cause" of this apparent delay. Some experts believe that the "delayed" behaviors are not due to a lower IQ (see the earlier discussion about the difficulties of obtaining an accurate IQ score) but to their reinforcement histories. That is, the experiences of children with such delays and the environmental reactions to those experiences may have been limited when compared to the "normal" population, causing the delayed behaviors.

When we speak of development, we refer to such aspects of human growth as self-concept, interactions with others (such as in play), physical skills, intellectual skills, understanding feelings, values, social skills, communication of feelings, and self-discipline. With regard to these behaviors, society identifies certain skills and patterns of behavior needed for a normal existence. Thus, developmental delays are said to be present when the children and youths' behaviors are significantly behind those of their age group. Virtually all children and youth identified as having autism demonstrate developmental delays.

If my child has developmental delays, what kinds of behaviors might I expect of him?

It is very difficult as well as unrealistic to generalize behaviors to all children and youth. Nonetheless, certain patterns are common among many children and youth with autism. Examples of physical behaviors include delays and regression in the ability to maintain bladder control (called enuresis) and/or bowel control (called encopresis).

Some age-related inappropriate feelings or behaviors may also be indicative of a developmental delay (they may also be indicative of other factors such as sensory deficits, etc.), including severe withdrawal from people, unrealistic fears, and/or temper tantrums. With regard to these feelings and behaviors, a developmental delay is inferred because excessive displays are rare in normally developing children.

Why doesn't my baby like to be cuddled? Instead, he seems to be preoccupied with himself, rocking in his crib, looking at his fingers.

One of the first signs of autism is a lack of "normal" responsiveness, such as cuddling, at an early age. Interestingly, this behavior pattern has been interpreted as an indication of being a "good" baby (the baby is not bothering anybody). Certainly, another parental interpretation of a child who is not cuddly or who fails to anticipate being picked up by a parent is one of concern. Although children who are preoccupied with themselves do not automatically have autism, a lack of responsiveness is a major concern and should be evaluated by a professional.

Will my child be able to live independently as an adult?

When provided appropriate training and experiences, many individuals with autism are able to live independent lives; many other adults with autism live semi-independently. That is, they are able to live outside of institutions and their parents' homes when provided close supervision and structure.

It is important to recognize that most persons with autism are able to acquire skills needed for independent living. For example, they become toilet trained, learn to use public transportation, and acquire other self-help skills needed for independent living, including the following:

communication: receiving and giving information in a meaningful fashion.

orientation and mobility: understanding where they are in reference to their environment and moving around in that environment.

hygiene: washing, tidiness, dressing, undressing.

sleeping: developing normal sleep habits.

independence: being aware of dangers, getting things that are necessary for daily living, eating in restaurants, using a telephone, and utilizing public service.

Why isn't Frank identified as mentally retarded? He fits adaptive and intellectual criteria.

Intelligence is commonly measured by standardized intelligence tests, whereby certain tasks and behaviors are assessed and compared with those of others of the same age. The scores of children and youth with autism often fall in the mentally retarded range. Further, their abilities to perform adaptive tasks are often similar to those of individuals labeled mentally retarded.

And yet, there are major differences between the two groups. For example, mentally retarded individuals tend to score uniformly low in all areas, while those with autism aften demonstrate variable skill and ability areas. Many moderately and severely mentally retarded individuals also demonstrate physical evidence of their disability (e.g., short stature); persons with autism usually give little such evidence.

What can I do to increase my developmentally delayed child's development?

In general, the chances of eliminating a developmental delay are not very good. However, by using techniques such as those described in Chapter 6, skills can improve. The likelihood of normal functioning for children with severe developmental delays is not high. While it would be tempting to lessen the harshness of this reality by making such comments as "all children are special," the fact is that all members of society have strengths and weaknesses. Our goal with all children, including those with autism, is to help them reach their potential.

But, my child is able to do some school work. Will he be able to improve in this area?

Depending on their ability and factors such as motivation and length of attention span, children with autism can accomplish school work at various levels. However, the school work must be within their ability range and apply to their personal *needs*. For instance, few would argue the importance of enhancing communication skills. To further illustrate, academics might include money use, time identification, knowledge of the days of week, development of prereading skills, and learning to paint. On occasion, particularly with students with higher functioning autism, more difficult school subjects might be appropriate.

SENSORY PROBLEMS

Sensory responses enable people to interact with their environment. For example, sensory responses (i.e., reactions) are made to sounds, visual stimuli, temperature changes, internal body sensations, touch, taste, and smell. According to some experts, it is distortions in under-standing these sensory signals that prevents individuals with autism from effectively relating to their environment. However, there is some contro-versy regarding the possible causes of these problems. Whereas some experts believe they are due to sensory problems, others believe that the condition can be explained as a cognitive problem.

Tommy gets very upset with certain sounds. For example, when the telephone or doorbell rings, he actually seems to get depressed. Why does this happen?

Over- or underreaction to sounds is not unusual in children and youth with autism. Such reactions may take the form of sadness, anger, or fascination. While some children withdraw upon hearing sounds, which they interpret as unpleasant, others repeatedly create sounds, such as scratching noises, and seem to derive pleasure from listening to them.

Sue seems to be fascinated and overly attentive to different objects. Is that unusual?

These behaviors are not unusual among individuals with autism. Some of these children and youth focus poorly on objects and, generally, seem unable to notice anything except outlines and forms; others focus with exceptional ability and attention on details and small objects. Other individuals seem to be distracted by lights or shiny objects. Still other children and youth engage in behaviors such as flicking their hands or moving their fingers near their eyes, watching things spin, or concentrat-ing on one particular aspect of an object such as a screw on an electrical outlet, or the knob on a television set.

Why is it that John can look at an object for hours while, at the same time, ignoring the loudest of sounds?

Some children with autism tend to focus on only certain things (e.g., the color blue), using only one of their senses, that is, visual or auditory. That is, they virtually ignore other environmental variables because they do not use, for instance, their hearing. This is called *stimulus overselectivity.*

The other day, Tom was outside in freezing weather without his coat. Can't he feel the cold?

It is not unusual for children and youth with autism to *seem* to ignore extreme ranges of temperature and/or pain. We deliberately use "seem" here because it is unclear if these individuals are unable to express pain or if they have different sensitivity thresholds.

Another interpretation of these reactions is that some children enjoy temperature extremes. For the same reason, some experts believe that some individuals with autism inflict pain upon themselves (i.e., to experience the feeling of pain).

At the other extreme, some children and youth with autism show great sensitivity to even slight degrees of heat, cold, or pain. As a result, a minor bump may result in an exaggerated response (i.e., what one would only expect following a major accident).

Dorothy approaches everything in an almost ritualistic manner. Everything has to be exactly the same way, each time. If her routine is disrupted, she gets very upset. Is this normal?

As with other behavioral patterns discussed in this chapter, ritualistic behavior is common among children and youth with autism. This desire for sameness has been interpreted as a way to gain security. While many of us share this feeling, some individuals with autism become extremely agitated if changes in their world occur. Changes can take many forms: morning routines, types of food ingested, utensils used, or even shapes, colors, and food smells. Many autistic individuals appear to experience high levels of anxiety when change occurs; others become aggressive.

I have seen autistic children and youth engage in bizarre body movements, such as rocking. Why do they do that?

Nobody understands exactly why individuals with autism engage in repetitive behaviors, referred to as *self-stimulation* and *stereotypical behaviors*. Some believe that autistic individuals find comfort in such behaviors as rocking (that's why we have rocking chairs!), jumping, or hand and arm flapping. Common self-stimulatory behaviors include:

saliva swishing (i.e., in mouth)

knocking knees against each other

rubbing eyes, ears, mouth, clothes, and/or objects

teeth clicking

tapping fingers against objects

pressing or twisting ears, nose

flexing muscles

grimacing

tapping feet on floor

manipulating objects

head weaving

light filtering

object spinning

hand moving (flapping, finger movements)

rocking

humming

squinting

Are there other strange behaviors that children and youth with autism display?

Absolutely yes! This population demonstrates a wide variety of the behaviors. For example, some children like walking on their toes; others have clumsy or expert finger movements. Still others demonstrate odd postures such as thrusting chests forward or inward. Some of these children, while apparently unable to clap their hands, can thread a needle!

Other children with autism confuse directions such as up and down, back and front, and/or left and right. These behaviors reflect the ability to follow verbal directions as well as imitate them.

Jack's way of approaching objects is similar to that of an animal. Isn't this weird, even for an autistic child?

Touching, smelling, and attempting to taste unfamiliar objects are not unusual behaviors for children and youth diagnosed as having autism. Some experts believe that their ability to receive information is impaired and that they rely on their other senses (taste, smell, etc.) to experience their world.

I know of an autistic boy who repeatedly bangs his head against a wall. Is this something I can expect my son to do?

Self-injurious behavior (SIB) is not common among persons with autism; however, it does occur, particularly in individuals who are also severely mentally retarded. Again, it is important to remember that the frequency and intensity of this behavior is crucial. For example, many very young children occasionally bang their heads during a temper tantrum. The self-injurious behavior to which we are referring is not occasional; it is frequent and potentially very damaging. It includes head-banging, self-biting, hand-chewing, self-scratching, hair-pulling, inflicting self-injury with objects, and ingesting inedible objects.

Results of untreated SIB range from minor injuries to permanent injury or even death. Various interventions, including those described in Chapter 6, are used with individuals who exhibit self-injurious behaviors.

What about hallucinations and delusions? I heard that these are pretty frequent among individuals with autism.

Hallucinations (seeing or hearing things that do not exist in reality) and delusions (believing that fantasy conditions exist) are not symptomatic of autism. Instead, these conditions are more likely to be associated with schizophrenia and other severe emotional disturbances.

SOCIAL PROBLEMS

Children and youth with autism experience major problems with social behaviors. Some experts believe that problems in the social arena are due to an inability to accurately perceive the environment because of sensory problems. Others attribute these problems to developmental delays, while yet others associate the inability to initiate and maintain satisfactory relationships with communication (speech and language) problems.

Children and youth with autism demonstrate a variety of social problems. Some children do not show affection; many have no friends of their own age; some appear unable to initiate intimacy; and many isolate themselves from others.

Frank simply ignores whatever I try to do with him. No matter how exciting or reinforcing my lesson is, he simply refuses to respond! What can I do?

It is highly unlikely that Frank is truly ignoring everybody around him, or that he is "choosing" not to respond. Acting as if he is in a world of his own, that is, being *aloof* or *withdrawn* from the world around him, is one of the most common characteristics of children and youth with autism.

It is important to keep in mind certain ramifications related to one's perception of Frank's behavior. For example, if we believe that Frank is choosing to behave in the manner described above, then we might react in a negative manner (see Chapter 9). If, however, his un- or underresponsiveness is seen as being due, for example, to a sensory problem, then the behavior takes on new meaning, allowing us to be more accepting and positive.

But, it is not only me that he ignores. He doesn't respond to other students, his brothers, or sisters. Why is that?

Again, if, in fact, Frank has a biophysical problem, the people mentioned may not appear different to him. That is, he may have limited ability to recognize and differentiate his behavior according to the people he encounters.

But, what happens when he encounters real dangers?

We have attempted to establish that it is extremely difficult for many children and youth with autism to understand and adjust to their environment. This includes all types of situations, such as dangers (e.g., being able to control factors). Hence, to avoid injury, many individuals with autism require close supervision and structure.

Sam never seems to play with his toys. Don't children with autism have imaginations?

Children and youth with autism interact with the world in a very concrete manner. If they have a ball, they may spend their time staring at it, or, perhaps, licking, or smelling it. It is less common for them to think of the various possibilities of "play" that a ball may bring.

When Sam reacts to a ball only as something to smell or touch, he severely limits opportunities for extending it to other activities such as playing catch. And, yet (there always seems to be exceptions . . . conditions that are contrary to the common rule), the vast majority of children like Sam can be taught to engage in structured play with peers and/or adults.

Sometimes, my son doesn't seem to recognize acquaintances, especially if we are in an unfamiliar environment. Is this common?

An inability to identify and respond to familiar people is characteristic of individuals with autism. The added confusion of being in a strange environment often compounds the problem. Even children who are responsive to certain people may seem unaware of their presence if they are outside the environment in which they are normally seen. Thus, a teacher may be recognized at school but not in the grocery store.

It is important to determine the manner in which a child gives evidence of recognizing others. Eye contact, blank stares, "real" stares, brief flashes of recognition, or contact for brief periods of time may be incorrectly interpreted as an indication of recognition.

My child continually plays the same record over and over and assembles and takes apart the same model over and over. Why is that?

While we cannot be sure of the exact motivation behind such behavior, doing the same acts in the same way seems to provide a certain degree of comfort. Whether in "play" or in the daily routine, these repetitive behaviors are common for children and youth with autism and pervasive developmental disorders.

Can I expect any other unusual behaviors from the autistic youth in my son's class?

Because of their difficulty or inability to communicate with the outside world, many individuals diagnosed as having autism display a wide range of behaviors. These behaviors may include, but are not limited to, aggressiveness, screaming, grabbing at things, running away, being destructive, and/or withdrawing from everything. However, it is important to remember that while youth with autism may show these behaviors, they can usually be taught to use more appropriate responses.

It's not just the inability to recognize others. He seems to be so cold . . . even to members of his family. Why is that?

As mentioned, failure to respond to touching or cuddling is not uncommon. Moreover, many autistic children and youth fail to demonstrate "spontaneous" affection. While this lack of response may be shown toward all people, some behave like that only with children of their own age or only with adults.

I don't know how to describe it, but Mei Ling acts weird. On occasion, she laughs or cries uncontrollably or gets very angry for no apparent reason. What causes such behavior?

Many children and youth with autism display emotional and social responses that are inconsistent, erratic or, maybe, nonexistent. It is impossible to judge what is going on in their minds; however, some experts speculate that it is related to an inability to accurately perceive the environment.

SPEECH AND LANGUAGE PROBLEMS

The terms *speech* and *language* are often used interchangeably. Both relate to the manner in which human beings communicate; however, they have different meanings. Communication involves the ability to deliver and receive understandable messages.

Language is the process by which we communicate our thoughts using meaningful rules and symbols. Thus, language disorders relate to difficulties in delivering or understanding thoughts based on the rules and symbols of language. Each language system has rules that help us communicate (e.g., verb tenses that indicate past, present, and future). Language symbols may take the form of words, or they can be concrete, such as in sign language, Bliss symbols or plastic symbols. In other words, language does not have to be orally communicated.

Speech, in turn, is the process by which we orally communicate, that is, by talking. Factors considered by speech professionals include articulation (the actual production of meaningful sounds), fluency (the flow of speech), and voice (the quality of our sounds).

Virtually all children and youth with autism or pervasive developmental disorders demonstrate significant speech and language problems. These problems affect not only their ability to express their needs, but also their ability to relate to others, their ability to learn, and so on.

Is it unusual for Jack to be mute? Is he voluntarily choosing to shut us off, or can't he talk?

As noted earlier, almost every child diagnosed with autism or pervasive developmental disorders has speech and language problems. Thus, research has shown that approximately 50% of individuals with autism fail to develop speech! Some speak just a few words and/or phrases; others are able to learn meaningless phrases, such as radio or television commercials. Still other children learn to communicate quite well.

There is little evidence to suggest that autistic children and youth choose to be mute. Indeed, this problem, *elective mutism,* is very rare among children and youth with autism.

When Don speaks, which is rare, he seems to be on the level of an infant. Will his language improve?

Many parents of autistic children first notice a problem in their child's development at the age of 2 or 3 when speech and language skills normally develop. In fact, speech and language professionals are often the first to make contact with children and youth with autism.

A variety of speech and language problems are demonstrated by children with autism, including Don's case. Some children speak in long, disjointed, and meaningless sentences; others utter occasional words; while yet others repeat previously seen or heard passages. The common link in all among these cases is that words are being used for purposes other than meaningful communication.

Could my child just have a language disorder, rather than autism? Isn't there something called "aphasia"?

Autism is far more inclusive than specific language disorders, including aphasia. Children with aphasia (a language disorder) may have an inability or difficulty in sending and/or receiving meaningful information. Although many people with aphasia demonstrate secondary social problems, most of them attempt to communicate with others—a behavior that is not apparent in many persons with autism.

Further, aphasic students may exhibit many of the same language and speech problems as children and youth with autism. However, the difference is the typical intent by persons with aphasia to communicate by other means than speech (e.g., gestures). Also, children with aphasia are more likely to play appropriately with peers and symbolic objects, to use their imaginations, and to understand more abstract concepts.

The way Patrick repeats whatever I say is extremely annoying. Sometimes he says the whole sentence; at other times, he might repeat part of what I say. What's the purpose?

Patrick's behavior is called *echolalia,* which may be immediate or delayed. *Immediate* refers to individuals repeating a word or phrase immediately after it is said by another person, while *delayed* echolalia is used to describe repetition of something that was heard earlier. There is little indication that Patrick (and other children with echolalic behavior) use speech to communicate. That is, Patrick may not be trying to express his needs or to understand the needs of others. More likely, his parrot-like behavior is a reaction to a seemingly unrelated environmental stimulus.

For many children and adolescents, echolalia seems to be most prevalent when they are in unfamiliar surroundings or are otherwise anxious.

I notice that sometimes Sam substitutes the word "I" for "you." Instead of saying "I want to eat," he says "You want to eat." Why does he do this?

Sam is demonstrating what is referred to as *pronoun reversal* or *pronoun substitution*. The origin of this behavior is unclear. Some experts think it is a learned behavior, that is, Sam is repeating what is said to him. Others believe this behavior relates to an inability to personalize communication. While reversal of pronouns may occur with older students, it is most frequent among those under the age of seven.

I don't understand why Bob can't use better language. His memory is actually very good. So what is causing it?

Many aspects of language supersede the simple memorization of words. Knowing the meanings of individual words and how they relate to others words seems to be beyond the capabilities of many autistic children and youth with autism. Thus, many individuals with autism do not grasp the ideas behind the words. An example of this deficiency is their inability to comprehend simple jokes.

Bob's language deficit might be similar to that of a computer. He can recall many words, but cannot meaningfully use the words on his own.

Bob is nine years old and still does not talk. Will he ever be able to learn to communicate effectively?

This question has two parts. First, it is unlikely that Bob, a nine-year-old, will totally overcome his language problem. Research suggests that children who fail to acquire language by age 5–7 usually continue to show communication deficits. However, as discussed in Chapter 6, alternatives to spoken language may allow Bob and other nonverbal children to communicate.

What other forms of communication problems are common to those with autism?

As mentioned earlier, a prime indicator of autism is a deficiency in communication. Accordingly, understanding and expressing language is, by definition, a major problem for children and youth with autism. For example, their vocabulary may be limited; their comments may be inconsistent with an ongoing conversation; their speech may be too loud; they may reveal various levels of pitch; or their speech may seem flat, atonal, and arrhythmic. Further, they may be unable to use gestures effectively.

Children and youth with autism may also have unusual voice inflections. For example, they may end sentences with an inflection that suggests questions, when, in fact, no questions are intended. Finally, individuals diagnosed with autism may be deficient in the ability to understand abstract language concepts.

My son doesn't use language, but he also doesn't use gestures, facial expressions, yes or no nods, or anything else to get what he needs! Is this common?

Gestures, head nods, and the other behaviors described are all forms of nonverbal (nonspeech) communication. This young boy not only lacks speech, but other methods by which he can deal with the world. Perhaps the severity of his condition limits his ability to communicate verbally or nonverbally. Or maybe he has not been trained to communicate. Chapter 6 presents techniques that are useful for teaching a child to develop communication skills.

UNIQUE ABILITIES

Some children and youth with autism possess unique skills that appear to be inconsistent with their disability. In the past, individuals with these skills were called "idiot savants" (meaning wise idiot). Such skills are highly individual and rarely relate to what most people consider to be "normal." In most cases, these skills are not functional. For example:

Aaron has an incredible memory. It seems that even the most minute piece of information stays forever in his mind. However, he doesn't seem to make any use of this skill. He will bring up the information in the most unusual times.

The autistic youth described in the above scenario appears to possess extraordinary memory. It is understandable, therefore, that his parents and teachers become frustrated that he seems to have a useful skill and, yet, is unable to use it effectively. Children and youth with this characteristic may remember things such as poems, songs, and commercials heard on the television, and yet be unable to attach any significance to what they remember.

Other unique skills shown by children and youth with autism include the ability to memorize maps and carry out complex numerical calculations. Finally, some autistic students can "read" extremely difficult words, but have no comprehension of the words they read.

Tom has the most incredible voice. Is this due to autism?

"Absolute pitch," for example, is not unusual among individuals with autism, nor are other outstanding musical abilities. This includes the ability to play a song on a musical instrument from memory after hearing it only once.

Alex can take apart and put together a radio. Does that mean he might be able to get a job as a repairman?

Perhaps. But these special skills are usually unique to particular situations. Often, special abilities shown by persons with autism do not generalize to different radios, or to the ability to diagnose and repair specific problems within radios.

SUMMARY

It is incorrect to assume that all the problems identified in this chapter are present in *all* children and youth with autism and pervasive developmental disorders. Rather, we have tried to compile a listing of relatively common characteristics. Further, just because a child demonstrates a certain behavior does not mean that he/she has autism. As mentioned in Chapter 1, the severity, pattern, and frequency of the characteristics must be considered.

5

Sources of Assistance for Children and Youth with Autism

Where can my child get help, and is it the best help available?

This question is not easily answered. A wide range of services are available to those with autism and pervasive developmental disorders, also called a "continuum of services." The continuum ranges from students living at home with their parents and attending regular education classrooms with no supportive help to placement in residential settings. Placement should be determined by evaluating the needs of the children and youth. Consequently, the chances of an autistic child being placed in a regular classroom, without supportive services, are slight. Such placements therefore, occur only occasionally with higher functioning individuals.

The purpose of this chapter is to review the roles of the people who may be working with children and youth with autism and to examine the placement and treatment alternatives that may be considered for this population. In considering these two matters it is important to keep in mind that because autism affects few individuals, only limited numbers of professionals may be trained to meet their educational, affective, and vocational needs. Moreover, treatment and educational programs for persons with autism may serve other groups of exceptional persons as well. Nonetheless, the staff will still have to make the adjustments necessary to accommodate individuals with autism.

What happens to the child who has been diagnosed as having autism?

Chapter 3 discussed identification and assessment. However, in spite of its great importance, assessment means little unless it tells professionals how to proceed with treatment, remediation, and educational programs. In this regard, placement decisions directly determine the dynamics of intervention and training programs.

What do you mean by "dynamics of intervention and training program"?

Determining the most appropriate placement and treatment options is based on a number of factors. In particular, parent and family considerations are vital. Hence, in addition to professionals' input, parent and family needs and recommendations must be taken into account. Parent and family member questions and concerns include: (a) Will our son live at home forever? (b) Will I be able to control my child as he grows? (c) What community resources are available to him? (d) If he goes to a community program, does that mean I am giving up my responsibility as a parent? (e) What will his brothers and sisters think?

Because a family's influence plays an important role in the child's ability to function in a given school environment, placement and treatment decisions should be based on joint family and professional recommendations and input. These may also change over time, depending upon a number of factors (e.g., child's needs, family changes).

How is the most appropriate environment determined?

The most appropriate educational placement, as stated in the federal law (Individuals with Disabilities Education Act), is called the "least restrictive environment." The least restrictive environment for students with disabilities is determined through careful examination of each student's needs and subsequently selecting the program(s) that most effectively meet these needs.

Conflicts between parents and school professionals occasionally develop due to different interpretations of how to most effectively meet a child's educational needs. Parents obviously want the very best program for their child. This goal is desirable for all students; however, under the least-restrictive-environment interpretation of the Individuals with Disabilities Education Act, public schools are required to place students in settings that are as close to those of nondisabled students as possible. This is not always the same as the best possible setting.

It has been recommended that our child be placed in a residential treatment program. One of the placements that is under consideration seems to be of a lesser quality than others we've seen. The problem is that the best programs are some distance away from our home and would lessen our contacts with our child. What can we do?

Placement decisions such as this one are particularly difficult for parents. In making such decisions, the following question is crucial: Does the quality of a program justify sending the child a long distance from home? If one program is only slightly better than another closer to home, the decision may be different than if the two programs differ significantly. In addition, children adjust to different programs in different ways. Accordingly, a decision on the best program for a given child can best be made after a child is given an opportunity to be involved in a particular program for several months.

What should parents consider when choosing educational and treatment placements?

Living with a person with autism can be extremely stressful. Hence, it is important to identify options that will serve both persons with autism and their families. In trying to make the right choice, answering the questions listed is helpful.

Is the family member with autism violent to self or others?

How restrictive an environment is needed to guarantee safety for the individual with autism?

What community and family resources are available for the child when he/she becomes an adult?

How prepared is the family to deal with sexual issues?

How effectively does the family deal with a member who has poor communication and human-relations skills?

How available and effective is child care for the family members with autism?

How effectively do the normally developing children in the family relate to a brother or sister with autism?

Are siblings given responsibility (too much?) for the care of the individual with autism?

Has the individual with autism hampered or significantly altered family recreational, church, or community activity?

Is the parents' age and physical health an issue?

Is the emotional health of the parents and family members such that they are able to care for a family member with autism?

Does the family's economic condition hinder their ability to care for a family member with autism?

What does the parents' age have to do with educational and treatment decisions for a family member with autism?

Parenting normally developing children and adolescents is difficult. However, in the vast majority of cases, the responsibility of being a parent lessens as children grow. That is, as children become older they are able to play with other children, take part in activities, join groups, and eventually live on their own. This "normal" developmental rearing process is not a reality for many families with an autistic member, however. In some cases, persons with autism need full-time care throughout their lives. Therefore, parents' age and health must be considered when planning for these children.

What educational and treatment placements are available and how are they similar and different?

While the placements discussed in this chapter differ in many ways, they also share certain characteristics. For example, the type of professionals who work across settings tend to be the same, generally including diagnosticians, teachers, principals/directors, vocational educators, social workers, psychologists/psychiatrists, speech and language specialists, paraprofessionals, and adaptive physical education teachers. In addition, residential programs also employ child-care workers and other support staff. A brief discussion of the roles of these individuals follows.

Diagnosticians.   The job of the diagnostician is to coordinate and participate in evaluating persons with autism. Sometimes, the diagnostician is a psychologist. In other cases, another individual, such as a classroom teacher, may be responsible for this task. Whatever the background and training of this person, he or she is responsible for collecting and evaluating information from other agencies and service personnel as well as from staff of the program conducting the diagnostic assessment.

Information gained from the various evaluations should be communicated to parents and other professionals in a clear, understandable manner. Children's specific strengths and weaknesses should be discussed in terms that translate into effective programs. Diagnosticians must be able to do more than simply identify students with autism. In order to be effective, they must be able to direct intervention and treatment efforts as well as ensure ongoing evaluations throughout the time a child is in a program. That is, diagnosticians are involved in assessing the effectiveness of various programs and students' overall progress.

Classroom teachers.   Most of the teachers responsible for educating students with autism have received training in methods and techniques for individuals with autism. Listed below are specific competencies these teachers should have in order to be successful:

behavior management techniques for students with autism

speech and language development techniques for students with autism

nonverbal communication techniques for students with autism

ability to develop curricula for students with autism

evaluation and assessment techniques for students with autism

ability to promote the growth and development of children in motor, social, emotional, cognition, and communication areas

social/affective programming for students with autism

understanding of the medical issues associated with autism

motor, leisure, and recreational programming for students with autism expressive therapy (e.g., art, music) programming for students with autism

daily living-skill programming for students with autism

self-care skill programming for students with autism

working with parents/families of students with autism

directing and supervising classroom paraprofessionals

vocational programming for students with autism

community and independent living programming for students with autism

This list is not exhaustive. The competencies that teachers need to demonstrate are many, because the needs of individuals with autism are many. Unfortunately, not enough teacher training programs prepare teachers to work with students with autism. Consequently, there remains a paucity of properly trained teachers and, as a result, many teachers must receive their training on the job.

Principals/directors of programs for individuals with autism.   Principals and directors of programs for individuals with autism play a major role in the education and treatment process. Principals are responsible for what is taught, how it is taught, and who teaches. These individuals are also involved in staff development, legal compliance, communicating with parents, and acting as a liaison among the various agencies serving students with autism. If a student with autism attends a school that also serves nondisabled students, the building principal is the same for all students in the building. However, if the program exclusively serves students with disabilities, the principal will likely be a specialist in special education.

If a child or adolescent is in a hospital or residential treatment setting, the school's principal will work with a general administrator, who oversees all facets of the program, including education.

Vocational educator.   Vocational educators have expertise in preparing students for postschool activities, including work. They teach such skills as responsibility, dependability, work-related social skills and hygiene, all of which are necessary competencies for students' vocational success. Specific "technical" skills may also be taught to prepare students to work in a sheltered workshop or for competitive employment. Vocational educators may also be responsible for communicating with potential employers and workshop personnel regarding autism and some of the specific characteristics of the disorder.

Social workers. Clinical and school social workers perform a variety of functions, but their primary job is to serve as a link (sometimes called liaison) between professionals, families, and community agencies. In addition, they may counsel family members and, on occasion, students with higher functioning autism disorder.

Psychologists and psychiatrists. Psychiatrists, school and clinical psychologists, besides being actively involved as diagnosticians, might also perform family and/or individual counseling. Such counseling might involve helping families or individuals recognize feelings and emotions that might be impairing their family relationships. Further, it is the psychiatrist's responsibility to diagnose and prescribe the use of any necessary medications.

Speech and language specialists. Teaching communication is the major task of speech and language specialists. Thus, they work with the individual with autism and may teach family members to help increase communication at home (see Chapter 4 for an explanation of the speech and language problems that individuals with autism may exhibit).

Paraprofessionals. Paraprofessionals play an important role in most educational settings. They may serve in a variety of roles, including classroom managers, classroom assistants, observers of behavior, and teachers of specific skills.

Adaptive physical education teachers. Leisure activity is an important part of everyone's life, including individuals with autism. Adaptive physical educators are specifically trained to develop and implement programs and to teach coordination and play skills to individuals with autism.

Occupational therapists. Occupational therapists may be found in any of the placement options listed below; however, they are generally not involved as often in regular education settings. Their primary function is to teach individuals with autism such life skills as self-care (e.g., feeding, hygiene, grooming, housekeeping). They may also teach skills needed by persons with autism to be successful in the work place.

Physical therapists.   Physical therapists develop individualized programs designed to help individuals with autism enhance their strength and coordination. This may include mobility training, exercise programs, and other physical activities.

What placement options exist for children with autism?

Placement for children and youth with autism is based on many factors. For students who are able to attend public school, the size of the school system, its location, relative wealth, and its commitment to education all affect the quality and quantity of educational services for students with handicaps, including those diagnosed with autism. It is particularly important that school districts have available professionals who are certified (i.e., licensed by a given state) and/or experienced in working with students with autism. School-related placement options fall along a continuum as described in the following section. Not all these options are available in every school district, however.

Regular education classrooms.   The regular classroom is often perceived as the "least restrictive" placement. However, for many students with autism, the regular classroom is not the most appropriate. It should be remembered that in such placements regular education teachers, who usually lack experience with students with autism, assume major responsibility for these pupils (although there may be *some* supportive help available). Consequently, students placed in a regular education classroom should be able to function with little or no special assistance. Since regular education teachers are responsible for teaching 20 to 35 students, it is unrealistic to expect them to be able to meet the needs of children and youth with autism unless these students are high functioning.

Before placement in a regular education classroom is made, a careful assessment should be made of a student's academic and emotional needs, and whether these needs can be adequately served in a regular education program. While many parents and professionals have aspirations of normal functioning for individuals with autism, regular education may not be appropriate for many of these individuals. Thus, such placements should be chosen based only on strong evidence that it is the most appropriate alternative for a student.

Does this mean that there is no possibility of regular education placement for my child?

For every "rule," there may be exceptions. Some children and adolescents with autism are appropriate for regular classrooms. In addition, some school districts may assign an aide to students with autism, making regular placement more feasible.

Consultant services. Educational and/or behavioral consultants are often used in public school "less restrictive placements," including regular education classrooms, resource rooms, part-time special classes, and self-contained classrooms. Since most teachers in these settings have neither the training nor the experience to work independently with students with autism, consultants serve to advise these teachers.

Consultants observe teachers and students, identify areas with which teachers may be unfamiliar, and offer teaching and managment suggestions. Consultants can also provide training (inservice or staff development training) to staff and/or parents. In the same instances, teachers with experience in autism serve as the consultants when students are moved to regular education classrooms and resource rooms.

Resource room and part-time special class placements. Resource rooms and part-time special class placements are designed for students who are able to function in regular education settings for at least part of each day. Resource rooms provide educational services for as much as three hours per day to (mostly) mildly handicapped students of different ages (e.g., 8- to 10-year-olds), grades (e.g., 3–6 grade) and abilities (e.g., learning disabled, higher functioning autistic).

Students in part-time special class settings attend special education classrooms for most of the day, but are integrated into regular education settings for a few class periods. Often the regular education classes include industrial education, art, music, and physical education.

Full-time or self-contained special class placements. Students in this type of setting attend special classes for the entire day, with the possible exception of lunch, recess, and physical education. With regard to public school options, this is the most restrictive settings discussed thus far. Students in this type of classroom are likely to be diagnosed as having autism or pervasive developmental disorders.

Some authorities suggest that only students under 12 years of age should be assigned to full-time, self-contained special education, and that there should be no more than 5 or 6 students in a class. These grouping recommendations are based on the developmental similarities of pre-adolescent students, which make instructional grouping easier.

Day treatment programs.   Day treatment programs typically follow a "normal" school schedule, although some have extended days. These programs are traditional, in the sense that they serve school-age children and youth from kindergarten through twelfth grade (in some states, special education services are provided to "twelfth graders" who may be up to 26 years old). Day treatment programs may be found in public schools or in separate (segregated) locations.

In addition to their physical location, the difference between a self-contained classroom and a day treatment program involves the additional support services available in day programs. For example, paraprofessionals (classroom aides), psychologists, behavioral consultants, and speech and language specialists are usually available to day treatment students and staff. In contrast, such resources may not be so evident in self-contained classrooms, which are usually staffed by a teacher and an aide, sharing support staff with other programs in the building.

When day treatment programs are housed in public schools, nominal integration may take place, such as shared use of lunchrooms, recess facilities, and so on. While this might seem attractive, there is a difference between *real* integration (i.e., social interaction between handicapped and nonhandicapped students) and settings where contact between children and youth with autism and their normally developing peers is restricted. Meaningful and well-planned interaction and integration can be extremely beneficial.

The primary benefit of day treatment programs lies in their ability to provide specialized and individualized programs for students with autism, including curricula in life skills, vocational training, and counseling. However, since day treatment programs for students with autism are not available in every community, this option may not exist for many students and families.

If we are going to seek education and treatment outside our community, should we wait until our son gets older?

This is a very difficult question to answer. If a child requires placement outside the home, we recommend that the action be taken as soon as possible, and that the child be returned to a less restrictive setting as soon as possible. Some research indicates that younger children find it easier to adjust to settings outside the home; however, this varies from individual to individual.

Also, younger children tend to have younger parents, who may have the energy and time required to monitor a placement and communicate with a school or treatment program.

What out-of-home placement options exist for children and youth with autism?

In recent years, there has been a major trend to reduce the number of persons living in institutions, resulting in increased placement in foster and group homes. These placement options provide 24-hour care for individuals with autism, while being more "normalized" than institutions. Services vary, but may include counseling, medication, and management techniques that might be difficult to implement at home (e.g., physical restraint).

Foster home placements.   Foster homes offer individuals with autism a family-type unit in a community. Residents live in a family setting while receiving special services (e.g., education, vocational training) as needed. Foster home personnel are usually trained to serve as "parents" of persons with disabilities, including those with autism.

Group homes.   Group homes are designed to serve small numbers of persons with disabilities. In some instances, such programs serve homogeneous populations, that is, they specialize in serving persons of similar age, ability, or diagnosis. (According to some experts, the optimal number of residents in a group home is one or two!) Since these homes are located in communities (as opposed to institutions), they afford clients access to the "real world" as much as possible and allow for a more personal and individualized approach.

Group homes rely upon community resources, including public schools, for educational services. Because of the varied and sometimes intense needs of persons with autism and pervasive developmental disabilities, effective community resources are essential for the proper functioning of group homes.

Some group homes have financial problems, which severely limit travel and activities. Families considering group-home placement for a person with autism should investigate the options closely.

Psychiatric programs and hospitals.   Psychiatric programs or hospitals are full-treatment placements, generally used on a short-term basis. A stay in such a setting might range from a few days to several months, sometimes longer. Decisions to utilize this type of program are often the result of out-of-control behavior of an individual with autism.

Psychiatric hospital treatment is usually comprehensive, although the primary therapy is medical (medications and other therapies are often emphasized).

Respite care alternatives.   Respite care provides a variety of services for individuals who are responsible for the care of a person with autism. Services include occasionally taking care of the individual with autism to allow the primary caregiver some relief time.

Institutions.   Although use of large institutions has fallen into disfavor as placement options, the reputation and quality of any particular program should not automatically be assumed to be poor. Decisions to place persons with autism in residential or institutional settings are complex and should include consideration of the following questions:

Are there sufficient staff (often called *client* or *staff ratio*) to serve the needs of individuals?

Does the program provide appropriate services and training, including living skills? recreation? education?

Is the institution integrated or isolated from the community?

Is the institution able to provide appropriate levels of attention to individuals?

Does the institution house clients in smaller units or cottages as opposed to large barracks-type living quarters?

Why is it necessary for my child to live someplace besides our home?

Residential placement is usually recommended as a last resort, often due to inadequate placement options (a problem that is not unusual in small communities) and the severity of a child's condition. According to the least restrictive environment concept discussed earlier, children and youth should only live someplace other than in their own home if they are unable to learn and live in a less restrictive environment.

Some students may have problems that are so severe that they are simply unable to live at home and attend a public school. Also, some family situations may contribute to a child's problems so that at least a temporary change becomes necessary. Thus, an out-of-home placement can sometimes provide a time-out from a very difficult situation, allowing those involved to examine critical issues that may be causing problems in the care and accommodation of a family member with autism.

Doesn't placement outside the home mean that I've failed as a parent?

One of the least productive reactions to dealing with an autistic family member is blame (see Chapter 7). It is very easy to blame children for their behaviors and emotions. It is also easy to blame ourselves for the way our children develop. Quite simply, what has happened, has happened! To examine and cross-examine the whys and wherefores only takes attention away from the main issue: How to resolve the problems at hand.

Regardless, there may be some shame (What will others think of *me* if Joe is sent "away"?) or guilt (Maybe this wouldn't have happened if . . .) associated with the decision to send a family member to a residential program. If these feelings are very strong, we recommend counseling. Many families share the same feelings and problems. Support groups or family counseling might be helpful. Finally, most residential programs recognize the need to include families, thus, they generally welcome family input and provide special services to parents and family members.

But, these feelings are very real. They are not so easily explained away. So what do I do?

We are not trying to explain "away" feeling associated with making difficult decisions regarding a family member with autism. Placing a child in a residential program after considering all the relevant factors is usually a sign of genuine concern for the child and his family! It is an indication that you have the child's best welfare in mind.

How do you know how it feels to be in this situation?

We only know what we have been told by others. But the point is well taken. Talk to people who are in similar situations. Ask the administrators of the program(s) under consideration for references (i.e., from other parents whose children are in the setting).

We also recommend taking the kind of actions typically done before making any important decision, visiting programs, asking questions of the staff and talking candidly with administrators. Questions relative to the educational/treatment program include: Is the atmosphere "institutional" or "homey"? Are the other residents similar to your son or daughter with respect to characteristics, strengths, and weaknesses?

Is there anywhere else we can go to find out about these feelings . . . about the types of placement available in my area?

The Autism Society of America (see Appendix for address) and its local and state chapters is one source that we strongly recommend. You may also want to contact the state department of education, social services, mental health, or mental retardation for the names of other organizations and programs that focus on autism.

What should my family say when asked about Tommy?

The answer to this question will probably vary depending upon the person to whom you are talking. For instance, you might decide to give more detailed information to close friends or relatives than to strangers. There is nothing shameful about somebody having problems. Thus, your response can be that, "Tommy is going to a school that can be more responsive to his needs."

An important message underlies your question. Tommy *has* a condition that requires care. His problems may be due to a variety of factors, most of which are described in this book. Avoiding this reality may create more problems. Fabricating stories and lying about Tommy's condition rarely helps and sends mixed messages to any siblings. Are you ashamed of him? Is he a "freak" because he has these problems?

A common misconception about placing individuals in residential schools is that the process involves locking someone away in a medieval institution. Most residential facilities are caring places that provide more than adequate educational, social, vocational, and living facilities.

SUMMARY

Selecting an appropriate (and least restrictive) placement for an individual with autism is not an easy task. In particular, it is important that the needs of both the person with autism and the family be matched with available program options and support resources.

6

Treatment and Interventions for Children and Youth with Autism

Autism is a lifelong disability for which there is no known cure. Children and youth who are identified as having autism will most likely carry at least remnants of the disorder throughout life. Thus, even high-functioning adults diagnosed with autism are often socially withdrawn, prone to using monotonous intonation in their speech, and perceived as "different."

The absence of a cure should not be interpreted to mean that children and adolescents with autism cannot make progress. The vast majority of children and adolescents with autism can and do make significant gains. However, such progress does not occur by accident; besides, autism is not a disorder that children outgrow. Rather, improvements result from carefully formulated training programs and intervention strategies. Temple Grandin, who was diagnosed as having autism as a child but who nonetheless managed to become a successful professional, gives credit to teachers and therapists for her gains: "I am deeply grateful to the dedicated teachers and therapists who worked with me. They were responsible for my [improvement], and their importance cannot be over-emphasized" (1988, p. 1).

This chapter presents several major treatment and intervention methods used with children and youth with autism, including education/

training, behavior modification, and medical interventions. The role of psychotherapy with children and youth with autism will also be discussed.

How can education and training be used to treat children and youth with autism?

Most experts who work with children and adolescents with autism acknowledge that education is the key to improvement. Because of the nature and severity of the condition, most individuals with autism are poor candidates for psychotherapy. That is, they are rarely able to discuss personal issues and concerns, including feelings and perceptions, with a therapist. Such activities require cognitive and language skills far beyond those of most individuals with autism.

Education and training have proven to be effective tools in working with persons with autism because they require few prerequisite skills and they provide direct intervention in areas of greatest need. That is, a child who lacks speech and language, has cognitive problems, and demonstrates a number of stereotypes (i.e., self-stimulatory behaviors), while being unable to discuss his problems with a psychotherapist, would be very appropriate for an "educational" program. Since his problems involve failing to do certain things (e.g., communicate, interact with others) while excessively engaging in inappropriate activities (e.g., flapping his hands for extended periods of time, thus prohibiting involvement with others), "treatment" would logically involve instructing the child in more productive and adaptive behaviors.

In the context of programming for children and youth with autism, education and training differ greatly from what is typically thought of as "education." Thus, successful methods may involve little in the way of traditional schoolwork (i.e., reading, writing, arithmetic). Instead, students may receive instruction in more basic areas, such as self-help skills (e.g., toileting, grooming), independent living (e.g., money use, use of public transportation), social and behavioral skills (e.g., greeting, responding and interacting with others), communication (e.g., verbally expressing needs), and vocational training (e.g., collating, packaging). Children and youth may also receive academic instruction, particularly to enable them to be more independent. That is, their academic curriculum will typically involve more basic goals and objectives than their normally achieving peers. For example, reading instruction may focus on teaching survival words, such as "men," "women," "exit," "danger."

Educational programs for children and youth with autism are usually very structured to enable children and adolescents to behave in more productive and adaptive ways.

What is meant by a "structured approach" to educating and training children and youth with autism?

Children and youth with autism tend to learn most effectively in structured settings. *Structure* in this context means that the program is consistent and predictable, it is organized, and it is designed so that students understand the relationship between their behavior and the consequences of such behavior. Thus, the various adults who work with students attempt to follow the same programs and procedures, relying on predictable and organized strategies. As a result, students learn that every time they engage in a desirable or undesirable behavior predictable consequences will follow (e.g., after successfully putting together a puzzle, a child is allowed to play with a desired toy for several minutes).

What are some of the elements of structure used in programs for children and youth with autism?

Several components of structure are common to programs for children and youth with autism. First, structure involves clearly identifying *individualized goals and objectives.* That is, unique expectations and methods are designed to fit each child or adolescent's needs. Accordingly, only materials, methods, and activities appropriate for a given child are used.

Structure also involves using what is referred to as *shaping.* Shaping means that a desired behavior is taught by instructing students in successive approximations of that behavior (i.e., teaching tasks step by step until a goal is achieved). For instance, if the goal is to teach a child to independently travel to and from his classroom and school bus, he is successively taught to travel greater and greater distances between his classroom and bus without assistance until he is able independently to make the trip. To be successful, shaping requires that positive consequences be used, that children understand what they are being asked to do, and that activities and materials are appropriate and within children's range of abilities and needs.

Another feature of structured programs is use of routines. Used to reduce uncertainty for children and to help them understand what to expect, this element of structure is particularly effective in enabling children and youth with autism understand and predict the happenings of their world.

A third element of structure involves arranging a classroom's physical environment to accomplish certain goals and objectives. For instance, a child may be seated away from a distracting peer, or floors may be carpeted to reduce certain types of self-stimulation (e.g., the noise associated with a child's self-stimulatory toe tapping). Moreover, classrooms may be designed so that certain areas are associated with certain activities. A child may learn that group work is done in certain areas of the class; that individual assignments are completed at a study carrel (i.e., a small work area designed for use by one student at a time); that vocational activities occur at a work table in one corner of the classroom, while free time takes place in still another. Assignment of activities to certain areas helps students understand teacher expectations, thereby reducing confusion about what they should be doing.

As students progress, educators typically try to reduce this basic assignment of specific activities to certain areas of a classroom. Thus, teachers assist students in recognizing that peer interactions can occur other than at a "group area" table in the classroom and that individual assignments can be worked on in a variety of places in a classroom. Nonetheless, at least initially, many students with autism benefit from the structure associated with careful planning of physical space and arrangement.

What skills are children and youth with autism taught?

As noted earlier, education and training programs are individualized according to each student's needs. Thus, it is unlikely that even students in the same classroom follow exactly the same programs. That is, their programs will involve different activities and curricula, depending on their needs. In spite of individualization, however, programs for children and youth with autism generally emphasize six basic areas: behavior and social skill development; communication and language skills; self-help and independent living; prevocational and vocational skills; academic and preacademic skills; and motor development. Educators will also frequently train compliance (teaching children to follow commands), particularly with young children and those with severe disabilities.

More and more, educational programs for children and youth with autism emphasize *functionality*. That is, students learn skills and behaviors that they can use in their everyday lives. For instance, toileting, eating, grooming, vocational, social interaction, language, community living, and similar programs are stressed, particularly with lower functioning students.

What is involved in training behavior and social skills?

Parents and teachers of children with autism and pervasive developmental disorders are particularly concerned about reducing unacceptable and deviant behaviors (e.g., self-injurious behaviors, self-stimulation) while increasing desirable behaviors that occur too infrequently (e.g., appropriate peer social interactions). Accordingly, education and training often include a great deal of behavioral and social skill development. Again, however, individual programs will vary in this regard, depending on students' needs. But since this area is so important and so basic to autism intervention, it constitutes a significant part of most curricula. A primary method of instruction for accomplishing this goal involves use of *behavior modification*, which will be discussed later in this chapter.

How are communication and language skills taught?

As with behavior and social skills, almost all children and youth with autism demonstrate speech and language problems. As defined earlier, *speech* refers to forming and using oral sounds (i.e., making and using correct speech sounds in communication). *Language,* on the other hand, is a general term that relates to using communication systems. Children with language deficits may lack spoken language, parrot back what others say, and generally have difficulty communicating with others.

Like other curriculum areas, communication and language programs are individualized based on students' needs. Thus, a student who has difficulty using pronouns (e.g., refers to himself as "you") would have a much different program than a nonverbal student.

For low-functioning and nonverbal students, speech and language programs usually start by training students to sit in a chair, attend to their teacher (i.e., make eye contact), model a trainer (e.g., touch their head when the trainer touches her head), follow simple commands (e.g., "Sit down," "Come here."), and avoid engaging in deviant behaviors. Not surprisingly, most experts agree that without these basic skills children and youth will be unable to profit from training.

Language training for nonverbal and lower functioning children may include object-use training. In this type of training, students are shown objects (e.g., ball) along with demonstrations of each object's function and cues to perform (e.g., "roll ball"). Such training expands children's language, preparing them for advanced programs.

Nonverbal and lower functioning children may also receive *motor and vocal-imitation training.* Students are trained to imitate the trainer's motor movements (e.g., child touches his shoulders in response to trainer touching his) and the trainer's sounds. Imitations of basic sounds may then be shaped into words. For example, once a child is able to say "ba" upon command, the sound may be shaped into "ball" and other meaningful words.

For students who have been unable to acquire spoken language, nonverbal communication programs may be used. Such programs may involve instructing students to use signs as well as communication boards, which include picture and object boards. These programs teach children and youth to communicate their needs by pointing to pictures or objects. For instance, a nonverbal adolescent might point to a photograph of a drinking fountain to express that he is thirsty. Augmentative communication systems, involving use of typewriters or computers, are used increasingly with some children and youth to allow them to interact with others. While communication boards and other augmentive communication systems are often viewed as alternatives to teaching children to talk, they may actually stimulate verbalizations. That is, some children and youth begin talking after being trained to sign, use a communication board, or communicate via a typewriter or word processor.

Children and youth who are capable of verbalizing also receive speech and language training. Programs include training children to identify and label objects and pictures. For instance, a trainer may hold up a ball while asking a child "What is this?" Students are reinforced (e.g., praise, desired object, food) for correctly identifying objects.

Finally, speech and language programs for children and youth with autism involve instructing them to use communication skills to deal with their world. That is, students are taught to use language to express their needs and to communicate with others. Thus, by making children and youth rely on spoken language, and by making language a functional tool, they become more adept at using it.

Speech and language training is carried out by a variety of individuals in a variety of settings. That is, speech and language training does not just occur when a language pathologist takes a student to therapy (more and more, pathologists conduct their training in the classroom or home). Communication training is so important and so integral to autistic students' development that teachers, therapists, and others provide speech and language training whenever they are with students. To ensure such a generalized approach, speech pathologists often serve as consultants to teachers, parents, and family members by suggesting procedures they may use to stimulate speech and language.

What are "self-help and independent-living skills" and how are they taught to children and youth with autism?

Instructing children and youth with autism in self-help skills (i.e., skills needed to meet their own needs in areas such as bathing, grooming, tooth brushing, hygiene, dressing, eating, toileting, etc.) and to perform activities that will allow them to live more independently (e.g., use public transportation) assists them in positively responding to their disability and, ultimately, in leading more productive and normal lives. Often children and youth with autism fail to acquire skills that normally developing children master (e.g., dressing themselves), thus making them dependent on others and, therefore, more "handicapped" than they might otherwise be. Consequently, education and training programs should be designed to train children and youth in those skills that most directly help them and their families live more normal lives. Parents and families should expect that at least a part of their children's education and training will involve independent-living and self-help instruction. Not every student will require such training; however, for those who do, it is an extremely important program component.

What kinds of prevocational and vocational skills are children and youth with autism taught?

As adults, many children and adolescents with autism can be expected to work in sheltered workshops for handicapped citizens, assume non-competitive employment positions, or seek supported types of competitive jobs (i.e., supportive employment). Supportive employment offers the services of a job coach or other assistance to aid individuals with autism in understanding and completing their work assignments. Not every child diagnosed as having autism will need to be in a sheltered workshop or other type of supportive employment. However, many will be unable to work in "regular" jobs and, therefore, need vocational training to acquire the skills required for post-school life, including employment.

Vocational training for students with autism is highly individualized. Thus, some students may be able to be involved in technical fields (e.g., computer training) while others require more basic training (e.g., learning to do simple packaging). Nonetheless, a core of common elements underlies vocational training: attending to a task without engaging in disruptive behavior; following directions; imitating motor movements (e.g., assembling an object in the same manner as a trainer); successfully completing match-to-sample activities (e.g., setting a table according to a place-setting model); successfully completing discrimination tasks (e.g., sorting various items according to their function), and accurately and independently repeating specified tasks for set periods of time.

As school-age youth with autism become older, they may be placed in vocational-education settings and otherwise assisted with transition planning and training. That is, their programs may concentrate on enhancing their vocational skills, in making them better able to enter work and vocational programs, and to live maximally productive and independent lives subsequent to leaving school.

It must be emphasized again that although not every child and adolescent with autism needs a vocational curriculum, so many do that curriculum in this area is a basic element of most students' programs. Similarly, most individuals with autism require transition planning and support when they complete school.

What academic skills are children and youth with autism taught?

To the extent that they are able, students with autism pursue a curriculum similar to that of their nondisabled peers. Thus, at the elementary level they may study reading, writing, arithmetic, English, spelling, social studies, and so on. At the secondary level, they pursue a course of study consistent with their abilities and interests. For students whose disability necessitates deviation from a standard academic curriculum, special academic goals and objectives may be developed. For instance, academics may focus on recognizing functional words (e.g., "exit," "poison," "men," "women," "bus stop"), writing one's name, and learning money skills. Finally, severely impaired students' programs may put little emphasis on academics. That is, rather than focusing on English, history, and math, these students may be involved in learning to communicate and interact appropriately with others, in addition to vocational skills, self-care, and so on.

What are motor skills and how are these taught to children and youth with autism?

Motor relates to coordination, muscle strength, and control and direction of muscles of the body. While every child and youth diagnosed as having autism will not experience motor problems, such deficits are common. Accordingly, many children and youth need individualized programs to improve their muscle strength, physical coordination, and motor dexterity. The content of such programs will likely be developed by specialists such as physical therapists, occupational therapists, and physicians; however, the programs themselves may be carried out by others, including teachers, parents, and family members.

In addition to programs designed to improve motor problems, students with autism benefit from physical education, leisure-skill training, and opportunities to interact with peers in game and play situations, as do all children. Such opportunities provide them a chance to develop new skills and interests as well as to apply previously developed skills to new situations (e.g., social interaction skills in a group play setting). Motor and physical activities should be included as a part of each youngster's education and training program, regardless of age or severity of disability.

What is "compliance training" and how is it used with children and youth with autism?

Parents and teachers frequently report that children and youth with autism lack motivation to learn new behaviors, avoid paying attention, and engage in behaviors that are incompatible with adaptive learning. As a result, it is difficult to determine whether students' deficits are a result of their inability to understand and complete tasks (e.g., student is unable to identify objects) or stem from their resistance to follow instructions (e.g., student is capable of identifying objects, but avoids doing so). Compliance, then, is a major issue in planning for and instructing students with autism, thus, it is frequently part of students' programs.

Compliance training involves using the following general method. First, a student is told to attend, in the form of a verbal or a nonverbal cue. The trainer (e.g., therapist, parent, teacher) gives a command and waits for the child to attend (e.g., eyes on adult, hands on lap). At this stage, behavior may need to be shaped for some. A typical instructional sequence of a command to attend follows:

Adult: "Tony, get ready." [Adult models attending behavior by placing hands on her lap and making eye contact with the child.]

Child: No response.

Adult: "Tony, get ready." [Adult prompts attention by touching child's hands.]

Child: No response.

Adult: "Tony, get ready." [Adult moves student's hands to child's lap, holding his hands until they remain in the desired location for two seconds.]

In the compliance training example above, the adult initially used a verbal request to get the student's attention. Only after the child was unable or unwilling to pay attention did the person use a prompt and, ultimately, physical assistance. This process is repeated (i.e., as an initial training step, children must demonstrate attention each time).

Subsequent to gaining children's attention, instructions to perform are given. At first, commands are simple and straightforward (e.g., "Give me blue"). While usually verbal, instructions may be nonverbal (e.g., signs) if required to assure children's understanding.

Compliance training commands are always presented in a hierarchical manner, starting at a level that allows children and youth to perform independently. Hence, children are given the opportunity to perform tasks without prompts. If children are unable or unwilling to perform correctly, increasing levels of assistance are provided. For example, if a child does not perform successfully on his own, a trainer provides a prompt or cue. If a prompt does not result in correct performance, the adult helps the child complete the task, a procedure known as "*put through*." Thus, *put through* means that a child is physically assisted in doing a task (e.g., a teacher takes a child by the hand and assists him in pointing to the correct answer).

An adult will often give a child a single command until independent performance is obtained. For example, a teacher might work with a student on "Give me blue" until the student is able to give the teacher a blue block on command independently. When this is achieved, the teacher may move to another task (e.g., "Give me red").

The obvious goal of compliance training is to have students follow directions and participate in desired educational activities. Compliance is so basic to learning that little occurs without it.

Is compliance training only used with children and youth with autism?

While serving as a basic instructional technique with children and youth with autism, compliance training is widely used with other types of disabled children as well as with nonhandicapped children. Coaches, for example, frequently use it with normally developing children and youth. Specifically, they provide cues for attention (e.g., whistle for attention), model a correct response (e.g., show the players how to shoot a free throw in basketball), and provide physical prompts (e.g., physically assist players in properly holding the ball). Thus, while not referred to as compliance training, this technique is a basic instructional procedure used with all children and adolescents.

Is compliance training only used by professionals who work with children and youth with autism?

Children and youth with autism who are noncompliant at school usually demonstrate similar problems in other settings, including home. Thus, parents and families often seek professional guidance in hopes of making their children more compliant. As part of these efforts, parents and family members may be instructed in compliance training procedures, thereby assisting their offspring in becoming more able to live successfully in a normalized environment.

The rationale for training parents and families to use procedures such as compliance training is that they should have an opportunity to assume active roles in the training and treatment of disabled members rather than merely being passive onlookers.

Is compliance training something every parent or family of a child or adolescent with autism should try to do?

Not every parent or family member of a child or youth with autism can appropriately or effectively carry out compliance training, tutoring, and other treatment programs. That is, due to such factors as interest, time, resources, temperament, motivation, and a host of others, some families and family members will not—or should not—serve as trainers. However, given the requisite interest and aptitude, parents and family members may use compliance training to facilitate autistic children's growth and development.

What does the term "behavior modification" refer to?

Behavior modification, also known as *behaviorism, applied behavior analysis, learning theory,* and *operant conditioning,* describes a set of principles and procedures for understanding and systematically changing behavior. Most educational and training programs and intervention procedures for children and youth with autism are based on behavioral principles. Similarly, most therapists (e.g., speech pathologists, occupational therapists) use behavioral procedures when working with individuals with autism.

How does behavior modification differ from traditional treatments such as psychotherapy?

Unlike traditional therapeutic approaches, which consider maladaptive behaviors as symptoms of underlying psychological and emotional problems, behavior modification views problem behavior as targets for change. That is, users of behavior modification do not support the notion that problem behaviors, including those associated with autism, are signs of deep-seated emotional conflict, but rather consider them learned patterns of maladaptive behavior. According to this model, therefore, developing maladaptive behaviors is no different from learning adaptive responses. For instance, children with autism may learn that they are able to manipulate their parents through tantrums or that kicking peers is an effective way to control others. Behavior modification principles are used to decrease maladaptive behaviors and increase adaptive responses that occur infrequently. In the preceding examples, tantrumming and kicking are viewed not as signs of underlying psychological problems, but as *the problems*, and procedures are subsequently developed to modify these behaviors.

What are some of the basic principles of behavior modification?

As mentioned, a basic rule of behavior modification is that maladaptive behaviors are learned and maintained in the same way as adaptive behavior. Further, users of behavior modification do not accept the theory that problem behaviors are caused by unobservable psychological factors (e.g., child's anger at a parent results in a permanent loss of language). Accordingly, maladaptive behaviors of children and youth with autism can be unlearned and replaced with more adaptive and functional behaviors.

As a result of this fundamental principle, behavior modification deals with specific, observable behaviors. Behaviors identified for change, therefore, must be overt (e.g., completing a vocational assignment, kicking another child) and measurable. *Measurable* refers to behaviors that can be counted or measured. Thus, instead of targeting self-stimultion for change (self-stimulation means different things to different people, making it difficult to measure), the target for change might be body rocking at home. Body rocking at home is a behavior that can be *seen, agreed upon,* and *counted.*

According to another principle of behavior modification, it is not necessary to assign a diagnostic label (e.g., autism, pervasive developmental disorder) to children or youth in order to treat them. Therefore, behavior modification practitioners attempt to improve behaviors that interfere with a child's adjustment without becoming overly concerned with how the child is diagnosed. For example, a child who avoids interacting with peers would be exposed to procedures designed to increase appropriate peer interactions. Whether or not the child had previously been identified as autistic would probably not affect the manner in which the program is applied.

According to behavior-modification principles, the effectiveness of behavior-change methods is not known until they have been tried. Thus, a procedure that has proven effective with one child cannot automatically be assumed to work equally well with another. Only by systematically applying and evaluating a behavior-management procedure can its effectiveness be determined.

A final assumption of behavior modification is that most behaviors are controlled by events and experiences that happen before and after them. A child's tantrums, for example, might be the result of parental attention to crying and screaming. The significance of this principle for successfully modifying behavior is great: If we can isolate the events that support a behavior identified for change (e.g., attention), behavior problems may be replaced with more adaptive behavior.

Who uses behavior-modification procedures with children and adolescents with autism?

A variety of persons use behavior modification, including teachers, parents, therapists, vocational trainers, and physicians. Although successful use of these methods requires training and guidance, one need not be a professional to use them. In fact, children often show the greatest gains when a variety of persons, including parents and family members, make consistent use of behavior modification.

What are the steps involved in using behavior modification with children and adolescents with autism?

Four primary steps underlie successful behavior modification procedures: (a) identify, define, and measure a behavior to be increased or decreased; (b) determine where, when, and with whom a target behavior occurs; (c) identify events that may be promoting or maintaining a target behavior; and (d) apply intervention procedures. As noted earlier, these steps may be applied by a number of persons, including parents and family members.

What is involved in identifying, defining, and measuring a behavior for change?

In accordance with the notion that problem behaviors are not symptoms of underlying difficulties, behavior modifiers attempt to change (i.e., increase or decrease) the behaviors that interfere with a child or adolescent's adjustment. Thus, *specific, precisely defined behaviors* are targeted for change. Examples of such behaviors include failure to follow parents' or teachers' commands, self-stimulatory hand flapping, or hitting another person. All these behaviors may be measured, that is, a teacher, therapist, or parent can count the number of times they occur and can share with others their observations and interventions without the interference of subjective interpretation and misunderstanding.

Why is it important to know where, when, and with whom a behavior targeted for change occurs?

As part of thoroughly understanding a target behavior, the person attempting to bring about a change must be familiar with the setting in which the behavior occurs and the circumstances surrounding it. For example, a child who is noncompliant only in the presence of a babysitter would probably undergo a different intervention program than a child who displays such behavior around a number of people. Similarly, an adolescent who is considered a problem only during the dinner hour or in school would be dealt with differently than somebody who tends to have problems across different times and settings.

What is meant by "identifying events that may promote or maintain a problem behavior"?

As noted earlier, behavior modification is based on the assumption that we learn from experience to do particular things in particular ways. Thus, a toddler may learn that banging his head against a wall is an excellent way to gain his parents' attention (i.e., whenever he bangs his head someone attends to him) or that hitting allows him to control a situation. Not all behaviors are so simply analyzed; however, identifying factors associated with the occurrence of a problem behavior is important. Accordingly, behavior modification involves attempting to uncover those factors that may be controlling a child's behavior and, subsequently, establishing the most effective and efficient intervention program.

What are intervention procedures and how are they used with children and adolescents?

The responses of children and youth with autism may be changed by systematic use of consequences. *Consequences* refer to positive or negative events that happen *after* a child has engaged in a behavior that someone wants to increase or decrease. For example, a child may receive additional free time in the classroom *after* she successfully finishes her daily math assignments. Similarly, a student may lose his recess whenever he engages in self-injurious behavior. Successful use of consequences requires that an agreed-upon intervention plan be followed each time a specified behavior occurs. Consequences can be of three types: (a) reinforcers, (b) planned ignoring (extinction), and (c) punishers (negative consequences).

What are "reinforcers" and how are they used with children and adolescents with autism?

Reinforcers are consequences that increase the likelihood of future occurrences of a behavior. That is, children and youth are rewarded for specified behaviors in the hope that such positive consequences will increase the chances that the desired behavior reoccurs. For example, a teacher may praise a child each time he verbalizes, or a youngster may be allowed to play a computer game at school if he completes an assignment within a specified time. In the preceding examples, teacher praise for verbalizations and playing with a computer for successfully completing an assignment function as reinforcers if they increase the specified target behavior.

Reinforcers for children and adolescents usually fall into three categories: (a) social rewards (e.g., hugs and verbal praise for desired behavior); (b) tangible rewards (e.g., edibles and toys for displaying specified behavior); and (c) contingent activities (e.g., recess and free time for compliance).

What is "planned ignoring" and how is it used as a consequence?

Children and youth with autism sometimes seek attention by displaying unacceptable behavior. For example, a student may get out of his assigned seat without permission to gain teacher attention or he may tantrum to control his parents' actions. *Planned ignoring* (extinction) involves systematic withdrawal of attention for unacceptable behavior followed by replacement of attention for desired behavior. Using this approach, a child may be ignored when she tantrums but attended to when she engages in acceptable social behavior. Extinction may not work with every child. However, for children who are motivated by attention it is usually an effective consequence.

How is punishment used to change the behavior of children and adolescents with autism?

Punishment means different things to different people. For some, it may create an image of a trip to the woodshed, for others, withdrawal of privileges. Related to behavior modification, *punishment* (or negative consequences) refers to any event that decreases a behavior it follows. For example, a child who reduces noncompliance as a result of losing TV privileges is said to have his behavior modified through negative consequences. Punishment programs for children and adolescents with autism typically involve response cost, time-out, and overcorrection. Spanking and other forms of corporal punishment are rarely considered appropriate forms of behavior modification punishment, and aversive procedures may only be appropriate in the most extreme situations, if at all.

What is "response cost" and how is it used as a negative consequence?

Response cost refers to systematic removal of rewards when specified unacceptable behaviors occur. For example, children may lose TV or other privileges for failing to abide by established rules at home.

How is time-out used with children and youth with autism?

Time-out involves removing children and youth from reinforcing situations whenever they display specified maladaptive behaviors. Time-out may require children and youth to sit quietly in a corner for short periods of time following unacceptable behaviors or otherwise restrict them from participating in reinforcing activities or being in reinforcing environments. One child was required to quietly lay his head on his desk for 3 minutes whenever he threw an object in class. Time-out has been used successfully by both professionals and parents. However, in spite of its popularity, time-out may not be effective with all children and adolescents with autism.

What is "overcorrection" and how is it used with children and youth with autism?

As a behavioral intervention procedure, overcorrection consists of two main parts, *restitution* and *positive practice*. The first, restitution, requires that individuals who disturb or destroy things clean up or otherwise restore a situation to its original state. For example, an adolescent who purposely throws food on the floor may be made to clean the soiled area. Positive practice, in turn, requires that a child or youth practice an appropriate behavior related to a maladaptive response. Thus, the adolescent who throws food may be required to transfer blocks from one container to another for several minutes. In this case, transferring blocks is an alternative behavior to throwing. Overcorrection is often a time-consuming and complex process; however, it sometimes offers an effective management procedure for children and youth with severe behavior problems and problem behaviors that have been unresponsive to other intervention methods.

How and when are aversive methods used with children and youth with autism?

Aversive conditioning refers to use of noxious or painful stimuli to reduce negative behaviors. That is, each time an individual engages in a previously specified, unwanted behavior (e.g., head banging), he or she receives a supposedly harmless, yet uncomfortable stimulus. Aversives include electric shock, foul-tasting substances such as lemon juice, and other uncomfortable stimuli such as water sprayed in the face.

Use of aversive procedures is highly controversial. Some professionals, parents, and advocacy groups strongly resist use of any aversive procedure, under any conditions. Others recommend use of aversives only in the most severe situations, such as in cases of self-injury or self-abuse. For instance, only in situations where an individual is apt to severely hurt himself by attempting to strike his eyes might aversive procedures be recommended. If aversives are used with a child or adolescent with autism, it usually takes place in a restricted setting such as a hospital or residential facility, and only with the permission of parents or a legal custodian.

Can medications cure autism?

As noted earlier in this book, there are no cures for autism. Thus, physicians are unable to write prescriptions for medications that will cure the disorder. Nonetheless, medications are sometimes used with disabled children and youth, including those with autism. While not cures, such medications may sometimes assist children and youth in dealing with their handicap. They are most effective when used in conjunction with other treatments such as education, training, and behavior modification.

What kinds of drugs are used with children and adolescents with autism?

Children and youth diagnosed with autism may experience seizure disorders; therefore, antiseizure drugs are among the most common medications prescribed for children and youth with autism.

Drugs are also sometimes prescribed to alleviate symptoms associated with autism. However, the utility of drug treatment in reducing symptoms varies from individual to individual. Much of the work in this area is still experimental.

Are children and youth with autism given drugs prescribed for hyperactive children?

Central nervous-system stimulant medications have become a popular intervention for children with attention deficits and hyperactivity.

These drugs are thought to stimulate concentration and attention, thereby reducing unnecessary activity, overactivity, and behavioral problems. Although experts are unable to explain precisely how the drugs work, they do seem to have a positive effect on some children.

Common central nervous-system stimulants include Benzedrine, Ritalin, Cylert, and Dexedrine. Side effects of these medications tend to be minimal, although there have been reports of appetite loss and insomnia.

Central nervous-system stimulant drugs are judged by many professionals and parents to be of benefit to a number of children. However, these medications have generally been of limited value to children and youth with autism.

What kinds of drugs are used to treat aggressive and acting-out children and adolescents and to reduce stereotypic behaviors?

Severe problems, including emotional outbursts and bizarre, self-stimulatory, stereotypic, and aggressive behavior, are often treated with powerful drugs known as *major tranquilizers* or *phenothiazines*. Specific forms of these medications include Thorazine, Mellaril, Trilafon, Stelazine, and Prolixin. A *butyrophenones* drug, Haldol, has also been used with some success. Although they may reduce disorganized thinking and hallucinations of individuals with psychotic conditions (e.g., schizophrenia) and generally help manage individuals with severe behavioral problems, these drugs are often associated with severe side effects, in particular, marked drowsiness, blurred vision, impaired motor performance, anemia, and tremors.

Less extreme emotional problems may be treated with *sedative* or *antianxiety drugs*. These medications, including Atarax, Vistaril, and Equanil, are sometimes used to reduce anxiety and hyperactivity and to induce sleep. Similar drugs, including Valium, Librium, Clonopin, and Tranxene, have anticonvulsant properties and, thus, may be prescribed for children who have seizure disorders. Sedative and antianxiety drugs tend to have fewer side effects than major tranquilizers.

What other drugs are used to treat children and adolescents with autism?

One medication that has been used experimentally with children and youth with autism is fenfluramine. Originally designed to treat obesity in adults, this drug is thought to reduce serotonin levels. As noted in Chapter 2, children and youth with autism sometimes demonstrate elevated levels of serotonin, neurotransmitters thought to affect sleep, cognitive ability, and appetite. Thus, by reducing serotonin levels in children with autism, fenfluramine is thought to improve behavior and learning potential. Results of the use of this medication are mixed: while some reports are positive, other applications of the drug have been ineffective in improving behavior and learning. Moreover, scientific studies of the drug remain inconclusive.

Dopamine antagonist drugs have also been used with children and youth with autism. As noted in Chapter 2, some children with autism have elevated dopamine levels (a neurotransmitter affecting motor activity, social behavior, and cognition), thought to result in problems similar to those associated with opiate addiction, including decreased socialization and increased levels of self-stimulatory behavior. Accordingly, drugs designed to reduce opiate action have occasionally been experimentally used with individuals with autism. Results have been inconclusive; thus, additional experimental work in this area is needed prior to wide use of this treatment.

Can use of vitamins and diet improve the behavior and learning of children and youth with autism?

Megavitamin therapy, including large doses of vitamin B, vitamin C, and various minerals, have been used to treat children and youth with autism. Although claims of improvement have been associated with these supplements, there is no solid scientific evidence to suggest they have any beneficial behavioral and cognitive effects. Studies in this area are currently being carried out. Similarly, there is no solid evidence that diets are effective treatments for children and youth with autism; however, research in this area continues.

What is the role of drug-intervention methods with children and youth with autism?

Medications can have profound impact on health and behavior. Accordingly, drug treatment must be considered a viable option for helping children and youth with autism. However, drugs are not a cure for autism and must, therefore, be used only to support other treatments such as behavior modification and education. Additionally, drugs are not appropriate or effective with all children and many drugs are in experimental stages. Consequently, any drug-treatment effort must be systematically evaluated and monitored. For every child or adolescent treated with medications, medical personnel, therapists, educators, psychologists, and families must work closely together to determine the drug's benefit.

How is psychotherapy used to treat children and youth with autism?

The term *psychotherapy* refers to any type of psychological or psychiatric treatment that is based on verbal or nonverbal communication. While different types of psychotherapy exist, they all rely on a discussion and/or interaction process; that is, they aim at improving behavior and mental health by means of having the person talk about personal issues and concerns. Thus, individuals are treated through discussions of their behavior, feelings, and motivations. Discussions may take place in individual sessions with a therapist or in groups of children having similar problems. With children or youth for whom talking does not come easily or who are too young to discuss their problems, play is used to allow them to express their feelings, conflicts, and concerns. With some forms of psychotherapy, therapists attempt to help children and youth gain insight, that is, recognize, understand, and accept their feelings and motivations, including unconscious urges and drives, and thereby gain improved emotional health and behavior. To achieve such insight and understanding, children and youth examine past emotional experiences, sometimes experiences of which they may not be conscious.

A basic prerequisite of psychotherapy is that individuals have the potential for self-understanding and insight. Therefore, attention is focused on making children and youth aware of who they are and why they engage in certain behaviors, including responses considered to be maladaptive. Based on the underlying assumption that positive change can only occur with accurate self-understanding, children and adolescents are helped to understand their relationships with significant individuals in their lives, including parents and family members. Self-understanding and insight, however, require cognitive, language, and social skills infrequently possessed by children and youth with autism. As a result most experts believe that psychotherapy has a limited role in treating children and youth with autism.

The exception to this rule is with high-functioning children and youth who may not only have the skills needed to benefit from counseling and psychotherapy, but may need such treatment as a result of being aware of their disability. As they become more aware of the differences between themselves and their normally developing peers, children and youth with autism may need to discuss their feelings and concerns with a therapist.

SUMMARY

In this chapter, we have identified and discussed major ways in which children and youth with autism are treated. In spite of the value of each, no single approach is complete or adequate with every child. Instead, the best treatment results when a combination of procedures is used. This requires cross-sections of professionals (e.g., educators, mental-health workers, medical personnel) using a variety of treatment approaches (e.g., education, behavior modification) based on the children's needs make the best progress. Additionally, to ensure optimal progress, parents and families must play an integral part in the treatment and education process.

Coping with Self-Defeating Personal Feelings That Can Prevent You from Dealing Successfully with Persons with Autism

The purpose of this chapter is to help you understand and, perhaps, control some of the self-defeating feelings and behaviors that may prevent you from working well with children and youth who have autism. Too often, speakers on television and authors of articles and books focus exclusively on descriptions and possible remediation techniques for individuals with autism. Rarely does the media discuss one major factor that is crucial to success: you, the parent or professional.

It is a common misconception among such speakers and authors that, if the "experts" give you the information, then you—the laypeople and professionals—should be able to follow the advice. Consequently, if the remediation techniques do not work, blame is placed on one of the two parties. It is our contention, however, that *one* factor rarely taken into serious account is the extremely difficult task of working with children and youth who have autism.

Many negative feelings may be attached to not being successful as often as we would like. These negative feelings might be frustration—because it is difficult . . . because they do seem to progress and then regress . . . or because they have those precocious areas and we think that we "should" be able to "fix" them—or guilt for bringing them into the world.

What feelings prevent us from effectively working with students and clients with autism?

We are here referring to any feeling and/or behavior that gets in the way of being able to achieve our goals. For example, anger, frustration, worry, fear, sadness, and anxiety are all emotions that, when severe, can prevent us from being successful.

But, isn't it "human" to feel these emotions, especially when it seems that we are constantly faced with failure?

It is natural to have these feelings when confronted with failure. Yet, some people seem not to let failures block their attempts at progress due to their personal philosophy about failure. Personal philosophy refers to the manner in which we think about failure, which is remarkably consistent within individuals.

It is also human to try to control these feelings, especially when they get in the way of our goals. In other words, we contend that we can control our harmful feelings.

How am I supposed to control my feelings when it is not (or is) my fault that my son won't respond to me, or when he continually messes up? How can I not have these feelings?

It is normal to experience negative feelings in reaction to the negative events that happen to you. The central theme of this chapter is that feelings are *not* caused by "bad" things. Rather, they are caused by your perceptions of those things.

For example, people react differently to the same event. In this regard, differences in our reactions to situations are no different from the fact that there are many different opinions about the same book or movie.

Even though we have different reactions to negative events, that still doesn't make it clear to me that I cause such feelings as severe anger or frustration. Can you explain?

Before explaining how emotional problems can occur, we want to emphasize that we are not assuming that everyone who deals with individuals who have autism has emotional problems. Traditionally, we have been led to believe that when something bad happens to us, the natural consequence is bad feelings. It is as if an uncontrollable cause and effect process happens. However, believing this (i.e., that bad feelings must accompany difficult situations) negates a very important component of human nature: our ability to think (often referred to as cognition)!

Thinking and feeling are closely related. We believe that thinking causes feelings. If we think something is pleasurable, we feel good. If we think something is obnoxious, we feel bad. In other words, we feel what we think. The fact that not all of us think the same about a particular event demonstrates why not all of us have the same feelings about the same event.

Does this explain why I feel frustrated when I can't get my son to understand me, while my wife only seems to feel minor aggravation?

Exactly! The kind of thinking that you might be experiencing is called irrational. Irrational thinking is a dysfunctional thought process, which may take the form of unrealistic demands, overgeneralizations, exaggerations, and unvalidated assumptions. Irrational thinking occurs when our opinions about certain events become facts to us. It is when our desires become our needs or our aspirations become a requirement. Opinions, desires, and aspirations are highly individual and when they cause an extremely emotional reaction (out of control) they are irrational.

For example, your wife may also not like that your son cannot understand her. Yet, instead of her believing (thinking) that he *must* understand her, she probably *wishes* that he would understand her; however, she knows that given his condition, it is unrealistic to expect such understanding from him without training or other intervention.

But this is not the way that I was raised. I was taught (and I believe) that it is not my fault if people treat me badly; and that anger is a natural reaction. So how can I change?

Even if we learned to think the way we do, with hard work, we can learn to think in new ways. This new thinking will create new feelings!

Let's look at a model for how we feel, known as the ABC model. The ABC model was developed by Albert Ellis as part of a psychological intervention program called *Rational Emotive Therapy.* (See the reference section for additional sources in this area.) The "A" in the ABC model is called the Activating Event, which is usually negative in nature (thus, the source of our negative feelings!). Later in this chapter, we will examine some experiences common to people who are responsible for the care and education of children and youth with autism.

A = Activating Event

Many people believe that it is the activating event (e.g., a child seems unable to understand us or cooperate with us) that causes our unhappiness (or happiness). While we believe that the event may *contribute* to our feelings, it is more likely that our perceptions or opinions about the event actually *cause* our feelings.

The feelings and/or behaviors (e.g., anger or frustration) that some regard as the result of the activating event is the "C" part of the model, the *Consequence(s).* The consequences that are of concern in this chapter are those that are so severe that they prevent us from meeting our goals.

C = Consequences

We refer to such feelings as anger, as opposed to aggravation; depression, as opposed to sadness; frustration, as opposed to annoyance, and fear, as opposed to apprehension. As a result, we engage in a variety of behaviors, including eating too much or too little; sleeping too much or too little; and experiencing an inability to concentrate.

You believe that when something bad happens to you, the "natural reaction" is to feel bad ("Who wouldn't feel bad if a child continually refuses to cooperate?"). This is when the most important aspect of problem solving comes into play: Your commitment to change your feeling! For example, how can you change your feelings of anger? Note: the question was not, "How do you want to change the Activating Event." Rather, the ABC model puts the responsibility for emotional growth squarely with the individual.

Your perception seems to be that "it is not your fault when people treat you or your child with autism unfairly or badly." Yet, you seem to be taking the responsibility for others' behaviors. In other words, why is it *your* responsibility that other people act in a particular way? Surely, there are others who do not react to you in the same manner. Some people *might* be more sensitive to your needs. Yet, others may perceive your (or your child's) behavior in a negative (individuals do perceive things in their *own* way) manner and feel justified feeling and behaving the way that they do!

Isn't this difference in how people react based on the way they were raised?

Perhaps. But regardless of the way we are raised, by recognizing response differences we acknowledge that there are different reactions to what we sometimes believe can elicit only one natural reaction. These different reactions comprise the major component of the ABC model—the B, or the Belief System. Belief systems refer to our perceptions or reactions to Activating Events.

B = Belief System

One way of understanding the concept of Belief Systems is to think of them as organized patterns of thought. They take the form of self-talk. Self-talk is the specific things that we say to ourselves that create our feelings.

Belief Systems? There are more than one?

Yes, hundreds of Belief Systems have been identified that create our feelings. People tend to use the same Belief System when they are confronted with a wide range of Activating Events.

When I get angry, depressed, or frustrated about my son's condition, I am not frustrated about his autism?

Correct! You are likely to react in a similar fashion (anger, depression, or frustration) with other Activating Events that you cannot control. For example, you probably feel the same way when people do not treat you in the manner you feel that you deserve. You may be using a Belief System called *Demanding*.

The *Demanding* Belief System encompasses an attitude by which you require, rather than prefer, things to be a certain way. Thus, the self-talk that occurs in a demander's thinking process includes words such as:

should
must
have to
need
got to

These words become sentences that leave the thinker with little choice but to be distressed. For example:

1. He shouldn't be autistic!

2. He must learn some skills!

3. I have to be perfect as a caregiver!

4. He needs to be different!

5. I know the way he should be educated!

6. I should be a better parent!

The above statements express admirable goals. However, when stated (and believed), they leave little option except for the person to be distressed: if he stays autistic; if he can't learn skills that a parent would like to see develop; if you make mistakes as a caregiver; if he can't be normally developing; and, if you are not the best parent or professional. And, of course, in most cases, these realities do not readily change.

What are my choices?

Your choice is to carefully evaluate your Belief System (i.e., examine what you say to yourself). Your task is to *prove* that the statements you make are true. For example, "should" people behave the way we demand? Given all their "unique" life experiences, would we really expect them to behave different? If people have spent their lives being rude, inconsiderate, or inattentive, do we *really* expect them to be different because we have determined it so? It is our contention, that while these statements may be preferable, they are not true—they are not facts.

I still think there is no other way to respond than the way that accurately portrays my feelings. What else can I try?

That is probably true. But your extremely negative feelings are created by the unrealistic beliefs evidenced in your statements. An examination of each of the "awfulizing" comments above reveals how inaccurate they are. This examination is called the "D," for disputation.

D = Disputation

Disputation is a process that can be both cognitive and behavioral. Its object is to minimize your harmful feelings by attacking untrue self-talk. For example, with regard to the destructuve self-talk used in the demands stated above, the following evaluations could be used:

Dispute 1:   Ask evidence of your thinking. Can it be proven that your son "shouldn't be autistic"? This is preferable, of course, but not proven because, for whatever reason, he is autistic.

Dispute 2:   Must he "learn some skills"? Given your son's personal history, it may be extremely unlikely that he will learn a skill (e.g., learn to talk).

Dispute 3:   Do you have to "be perfect as a caregiver"? Can you, or anyone, be perfect as caregiver, or as anything else for that matter?

Dispute 4:   Does he "need to be different"? Most parents and professionals would probably wish for individuals not to have autism. But they do not need to be "different" ("normal?"); they have lived their lives being "different," just as you and I have.

Dispute 5:   Do you really "know the way that he should be educated"? You may be qualified to provide input about a particular student's education given everything you know about him. Yet, it is highly unlikely that anyone knows for sure what will absolutely, positively work for any individual, and what that individual needs.

The emotional consequences of the statements you make create your unhappiness. In addition, failure to examine the reality of these statements ensures your unhappiness.

It sounds good, but isn't it easier said than done?

Absolutely! Again, the purpose of this chapter is not to suggest that change is easy. It is very difficult! However, the alternative is to continue believing things that simply are not true . . . they cannot be validated . . . these beliefs are only your unvalidated opinions.

What other Belief Systems do we have?

The *Awfulizing* Belief System involves gross negative exaggerations. Thus, people who use such systems use overgeneralizations such as, "totally bad" or "absolutely horrible." In other words, they make a practice of "making a mountain out of a mole hill." *Awfulizers* believe that things are "totally bad." They also tend to be "whiners." Rather than dealing with problems, they prefer to believe that the world is too difficult to deal with and that, therefore, they have to endure it (no matter how difficult). The self-talk that is part of their vocabulary includes the following descriptions:

awful
horrible
terrible
unbearable
catastrophe
poor me

These words become part of our working philosophy, and drive our emotions into unhappiness. Examples of unrealistic sentences using these words include:

1. It's awful that he is autistic.

2. It's horrible that I had an autistic child.

3. It's terrible that he won't do what I ask.

4. My life is now unbearable.

5. Each time that a problem occurs, it is truly a catastrophe.

6. Poor me! Why does this always have to happen to me!

People with this kind of Belief System consider disappointments as not mere disappointments, but as indicators of the worst (100% bad!) things that could possibly happen. For example, "My son with autism refuses to do what I ask. I can't believe anything worse can happen!" Certainly, for most people, this experience is *not the worst thing that can happen.*

Can't some things be absolutely, totally bad?

Some things can certainly be unpleasant, very unpleasant. But, absolutely, totally bad? Probably not, because the worst thing that can happen to anyone can usually be topped by something worse. No matter how bad an Activating Event, it can always be worse. Can you *imagine* how things could be worse? Although this may not be a major comfort, it does reflect reality.

There are many people with disabilities, with terminal illnesses, and people who have otherwise been dealt a "losing hand," who do not feel and act as if their world has been taken apart. If these Activating Events *caused* the hardships, all of these people would react in a similar manner. More likely, these people believed that the events were extremely unpleasant, but tolerable.

Let's now examine some possible disputations for the "awfulizing" statements noted above:

Dispute 1: Is it *awful* that he has autism? Although it certainly is not pleasurable for him or you, it cannot be proven that it is 100% awful. Both you and the person with autism have and will experience many "unawful" times. This certainly minimizes your opinion that his condition is totally awful.

Dispute 2: "It's horrible that I had an autistic child" is also an overexaggeration if by *horrible* you are describing the "worst thing that could have happened to you," as opposed to an event that is less than you had desired. Clearly, worse things could have happened. Your child could have been more severely handicapped, your other children could have been severely handicapped, or you could have died during childbirth. These are all events that could have been more horrible. The purpose of presenting such realities is not to be macabre; rather, it is to make you look at the possible events that could have occurred to make your life more "horrible."

Dispute 3: Probably, it is also not terrible that he will not do what you ask. He has not always done (and we imagine that others have not always done) what you have requested in the past and it has not been so terrible. You lived through the disappointment even though you may not have thought that it was possible, *and,* you adapted to the situation.

Dispute 4: That one's life is "unbearable" is a common "awfulizing" remark. Is it so unbearable that you would commit suicide over it? If you are seriously considering suicide, we recommend that you seek professional help. If not, how do the catastrophes in your life compare to those of others? Think of those with incurable diseases, the homeless, or those who have lost their homes because of financial difficulties. Are the lives of

all those people unbearable? How do you account for many of the sur-
vivors of concentration camps whose lives are not unbearable? How does
the condition of your life compare?

Dispute 5:   When one believes that "each time a problem occurs, it is
truly a catastrophe," one obviously uses the word *catastrophe* very
loosely. Unpleasant events, such as not getting your way all the time, does
not fit the definition of catastrophe. You are just choosing to use it
incorrectly.

Dispute 6:   Finally, the "poor me's" are usually overreactions to unpleasant events. Bad things do happen. Because they happen to you does not
make you "poor." It is clear that there is little evidence of the other over-
generalization "everything always happens to me." Everything does not
happen to anyone, including you!

But these events always seem so important when they occur. Is there a way that will help me look at the realistic side of things?

One technique that might help is to ask yourself how you will feel
about the event tomorrow, next week, next month, or next year. The
answer is that you will probably feel that it is less "terrible." Why is that
so?
Think of some previous "horrible" events that no longer seem so
disastrous. How do you describe the event now? Can you say the same
things *now* about the current event rather than wait for time to elapse?

Sometimes when I feel bad, I tend to avoid unpleasant events. Is that normal?

It is very normal to avoid negative events. However, avoiding events
rarely solves the problem. In fact, it might lead to more avoidance, by
providing temporary relief.

But sometimes it is easier to avoid dealing with my autistic son and to avoid working so hard when I know that the results are most likely going to be less than what I want! Don't you see?

It is easier! Yet, is it what you want? Are you satisfied that you no
longer spend the time you would like to with your son? Is the avoidance of
work getting the desired results?

What can I do to overcome this avoidance?

Choose the correct, but undesirable behavior! Interestingly, most people report that when they engage in the uncomfortable behavior, the emotional results are rarely as "horrible" as they imagined!

In fact, while some believe that the way to approach an undesired event is in small doses, others suggest that the best way is to force yourself to fully confront the event. They believe that by doing it little by little, you are reinforcing the notion that it is a horrible event and that the only way to deal with it is with trepidation.

In my situation, I don't think I demand or "awfulize." I just feel like a terrible parent (teacher, friend, whatever) whenever things don't go right. How about you?

The reaction you describe is not uncommon. However, others will respond by blaming others, including teachers, school staff, and so forth.

Both of these ways of dealing with a child with autism are indicative of the *Rating* Belief System, which involves evaluating human worth, whether your own or that of others. It suggests that an event (a behavior or set of behaviors) comprises the essence of an individual. Consequently, if somebody does something "bad," he or she is "bad."

But isn't that what self-concept is all about? Doesn't it involve the way that we are perceived by others?

An unhealthy approach to evaluating self-concept or self-worth is to base it on the perspectives of others. Who is to say that their evaluations, or yours for that matter, are accurate? Further, if these evaluations are based on a behavior, a mistake for instance, doesn't that suggest that human beings are infallible? It is important to remember that almost all people are fallible: consequently, they do make mistakes.

When individuals blame themselves or others for a misdeed, they are taking a relatively self-righteous role. They are saying (believing) that they or others do not have the right to err. To them, to err is not human, and to forgive could only be Divine.

I don't understand. I know that I feel good when I do something well. Isn't it natural that I also feel good when my autistic child does something well? And, doesn't this also apply when my child or I do something poorly?

It is appropriate to feel good when good things happen. But it is different when you think that you are a good person because you do a good thing. Further, it cannot be proven that if you do something bad, you become a bad person. To suggest that a person is good or bad based on a few behaviors is to overgeneralize. Some of the relevant self-talk words include:

worthless
retard (or other name)
stupid
irresponsible
rotten

When these words are used to describe you or others, they will probably result in debilitating feelings, including depression, guilt, shame, or anger. They might be used in the context of the following self-talk:

1. Bobby hasn't improved at all. That teacher is absolutely worthless!

2. He is such a retard. He doesn't know how to behave.

3. I didn't do that well. I am so stupid.

4. He's late again. He is totally irresponsible.

5. What a rotten guy. He is so mean to my son!

Although it is understandable that we become disappointed when unpleasant events occur, there is little evidence to support the above self-talk evaluations. For example, consider the following disputations:

Dispute 1: Is the teacher's worth based entirely on his ability to work with Bobby? Does he do well with other students? Have others been more successful with Bobby? Can one accurately evaluate the teacher's worth based on his interactions with Bobby? Even if he is not as successful with Bobby as is possible, will this faulty evaluation of his worth get what you need: Good communication with this teacher to improve Bobby's skills?

Dispute 2: To describe an individual as a retard (even if the individual has been clinically assessed as having mental retardation) because of inappropriate or certain other behaviors is a hasty and unfair generalization. It unfairly places the person in an unattractive category and contends that if people are different, they should be degraded.

Dispute 3:   People who say they are stupid when they do not do well are suggesting that they must do well in everything not to be stupid. Do they become smart when they do some things well? This attitude takes away the reality of fallibility that is integral to our humanness. Can anyone honestly state they they are infallible?

Dispute 4:   To suggest that somebody is totally irresponsible because he or she is late (again) ignores or minimizes other qualities. Even if the person is not very responsible, does that make them a horrible human being?

Dispute 5:   It is tempting to think of somebody as "a rotten guy" because he is mean to your son. The fact that your son has autism might add ammunition to your emotional arsenal. Not everybody knows how to effectively interact with individuals with autism and, while that is unpleasant, it gives little credence to the evaluation of a rotten essence!

I work very hard at what I do. I carefully plan activities for my child, and, I can honestly say that I am at least adequate in everything that I do. Or, I just won't do it!! So?

It is too bad if you avoid what could be pleasant events because you are less than adequate at them. Keep in mind that the evaluation of adequacy means different things to different people. For example, adequacy for some golfers might be 100; others might define it as 75, and might consider quitting the game if they score in the 80s!

It is not inappropriate to strive for excellence. However, placing the pressure of perfection on yourself may severely limit your opportunities for progress and enjoyment.

Okay, but does all of this understanding about what creates my upset feelings help me with my problem(s)?

Simply understanding your problem does not stop your feelings from occurring. You have to practice the disputations when the Activating Events occur. This is called the "E" or the Effect.

$$E = Effect$$

The Effect is your commitment to change your negative feelings; the hard work and practice needed to make the desired change. Behavioral principles such as positive reinforcement can often help ensure that your realistic self-talk is practiced. That is, rewards or punishments are applied when the self-talk is used (or not used).

How can I apply the ABC process?

On a sheet of paper, complete the components of the model. That is, list your A, B, C, and D elements (we assume you have an understanding of the ABCD concepts; if you need more information, see the reference section). Practice your "D" statements when you feel distressed. Ask yourself the following questions in order to facilitate the process:

1. A = The Activating Event (What happened?)

2a. C = Consequences (What emotions or behaviors do you want to change?)

2b. How does the feeling affect you?

2c. How do you want to change this feeling?

3a. B = Belief System (List the self-talk that makes you . . .)

3b. What System is used?

4. D = Disputations (Give evidence that your Beliefs are true.)

5. E = Effect (How am I going to make needed changes?)

Let's examine two of the most damaging emotions: anger and frustration. They are damaging because they interfere with the caregiver's long-term goals of creating an active, loving, exciting, and enriching learning environment for children and youth with autism. Once a self-defeating feeling (behavior) is exhibited, it is extremely difficult to regain the composure necessary to achieve the above goals.

A number of events make us feel upset under any circumstances, and particularly when faced with the arduous task of continually dealing with a handicapped individual. Caregivers report that the following are only a few of the things that make this relationship difficult:

Family members who do not understand my situation

Lack of support from administration, etc.

Bad behavior of children, clients

My inability to help certain youth

People who do not care

Lack of client (child) progress

Caregivers who are "unprofessional"

These problems can be debilitating if a person's self-talk is unrealistic. The following are descriptions of how Frank, and later Susan, can use the ABC model to deal with their problems.

Problem #1: Dealing with a Lack of Support

Frank is a special education teacher who works with students with severe handicaps. He is considered to be good with his students, and has been highly evaluated by his superiors. During the last school year, Frank's principal, Mr. Smith, placed three students over the state's limit in Frank's classroom. The additional students put an unfair burden on Frank, which was detrimental to the students' education. Frank protested and Mr. Smith promised that if Frank did not "make waves," he would hire another special-education teacher, which would mean underenrollment for Frank the next year. Frank agreed not to cause any problems.

This year, Frank's class is still three students over the maximum and there is little indication that it will change. Frank complained to Mr. Smith who responded that he had not been able to get the necessary funds. "Besides," he added, "since you did such a nice job last year with your class size, I didn't think it would be a problem this year." Frank reminded Mr. Smith of their agreement to which Mr. Smith responded that Frank should stop whining and that if he did not like his job, he could look for another one. He also reminded Frank that he agreed to the extra numbers the previous year; "Nobody put a gun to your head." Frank became extremely angry. He could not concentrate on preparing his lessons and he became short-tempered with his students and family. He could not sleep well. He began to consider quitting his job.

1. A = The Activating Event (What happened?)
Mr. Smith broke an agreement with me. He promised to reduce my class size. Heck, I wouldn't even mind if he just lowered it to meet the state regulations.

2a. C = Consequences (What emotions or behaviors do you want to change?)

Anger. Also, resentment, frustration, and depression. (Frank chose *one* emotion to work on: Anger.)

2b. How does the feeling affect you?

"I can't sleep . . . can't concentrate. I feel like hitting Mr. Smith or telling him what a creep he is. It seems like I lose my temper too quickly with my students. I'd rank my anger at 90 (out of 100). I'm "losing it," and this is just not "like me.""

2c. How do you want to change this feeling?

"This is tough. I know I'm right. I just can't do anything because of these feelings. I would like to be able to control myself. Perhaps, a 60? I don't want to stop caring about this, but I'm also not getting anything done and I'm being a jerk with my students and family. They don't understand me."

3a. B = Belief System (List the self-talk that makes you angry.)

"The jerk lied to me. He has no right to do that!"

"Principals shouldn't do that!"

"I'm going to do what I can to get that bum fired!"

"Poor me. I can't stand this job anymore." (Not appropriate for this problem! Does this statement make you angry or depressed?)

"Everybody should stand up and support me on this one! They don't care and they deserve what they will get." (Frank gives no realistic beliefs.)

3b. What System is used?

Demanding. Some rating, but primarily demanding.

4. D = Disputations (Give evidence that your Beliefs are true.)

"How provable is it? Well, he did lie to me. I guess others have lied to me before and I've handled it. I'm old enough to realize that people do lie, even teachers! I wish they wouldn't, but that's the way it is."

"Principals are people, and many people do look out for their own best interests. I don't know why I let him sucker me . . . he's done it before. I'd prefer that he be honest."

"Maybe he was looking out for his own best interests, maybe even the students'. I wish he knew a better way to communicate, even though I know that he's always been this way."

"It would be nice if he would uphold his end of the bargain; because I upheld mine! Unfortunately, things don't always work out that way."

"Even though he *could* have acted differently, I really have little evidence that he *should* have. I don't know his pressures. Maybe he was telling me the truth, and he simply doesn't have the communication skills to effectively tell me, and don't I know that!"

"I guess I'm really asking *him* to be a better person because *I* want him to be one. Sounds like I'm doing the same thing he's doing. Maybe, *I* can't have what I want all of the time. Even though it was promised!"

"I could probably get others to agree that I was wronged. Yet, does that prove it without a shadow of a doubt?"

"I could probably be reasonably happy in my job with the extra kids. If I can't be happy, I might look for another job. What choices *do* I really have? To let him destroy my home life and job, or for me to tolerate his behavior?"

"My anger is not getting me what I want! My job and relationships are suffering. Mr. Smith is avoiding me. In fact, if I get my way through a demonstration of anger power, *he* just might figure out a way to get back at me!"

5. *E = Effect (How am I going to make needed changes?)*

"I am going to try to accept my principal's dishonesty. I do not like it, but I do like my job and this community. His lies are really only an annoyance. I am going to try different avenues, in an assertive yet nondemanding way, to get my class size lowered." (Notice: Frank is *not* trying to get the Activating Event altered.)

"The next time he lies, I am not going to be surprised. I will simply not react with great expectations to his statements. I will try to avoid future agreements with him. If I fail to accept his dishonesty and get angry with him again, my *punishment* (because I am not practicing my rational thinking) will be to ask him if there are any committees or extra work he would like me to do for him."

Problem #2: Inability to Help Certain Youth

Susan has been attempting to help Joe, her son with autism, learn some simple communication skills using a new program. The program involves training gestures that will allow Joe to make some of his needs known. At first, Joe seemed to be fairly successful at learning the program, but he continually regressed, sometimes to the point of losing all his skills. Susan feels she can't work with Joe; no matter what she tries, her efforts fail. She is very distressed at her inability to solve this dilemma.

1. A = The Activating Event (What happened?)
"Joe is just a constant failure. He cannot learn to communicate. No matter what I try, he still fails to learn."

2a. C = Consequences (What emotions or behaviors do you want to change?)
Frustration. (In this case, Susan had only one feeling about the event.)

2b. How does the feeling affect you?
"I find myself spending too much time trying to solve this puzzle. I find myself wanting to avoid Joe. This is getting in the way of my work with other family members, my social involvements, even my job. I would rate my frustration as a 75 out of 100."

2c. How do you want to change this feeling?
"I would like to lower my frustration to 40. I want to be able to continue working with Joe and regain perspective on the other aspects of my life."

3a. B = Belief System (List the self-talk that makes you . . .)
"I can't stand the fact that he isn't learning from me. This is the worst thing that has happened to me. Maybe he needs a better parent."
"He should know how to communicate by now!"
"*Everyone* can learn."
"There must be a way for me to reach him."

3b. What System is used?
Awfulizing, demanding, and rating.

4. D = Disputations (Give evidence that your Beliefs are true.)
"First and foremost, I seem to be telling myself that Joe, a severely autistic boy, should *know* better! Common sense would indicate that if he did know better, he wouldn't be disabled! I'm not accepting conditions the way they are."
"I seem to be putting an awfully big responsibility upon myself. I would prefer to be successful in all of my endeavors. But it seems grandiose to expect that I am some sort of supermom."
"I know from my experiences, and the experiences of others, that everybody doesn't learn at the same speed or using the same program."
"This is really an unfortunate time that I am going through. But it certainly isn't the worst thing that has ever happened to me."

"There might be (not necessarily "is") a way to teach Joe. I am going to continue to try."

"Joe isn't doing this 'to me'; rather, this situation is occurring because he can't help it."

5. *E = Effect (How am I going to make these changes?)*

"Even though it is frustrating for me to watch Joe slip each time, I will try to be more tolerant and accepting of him and myself. Since my goal is to teach Joe, my previous unrealistic feelings were only getting in the way of that goal (which may never be met). As a 'punishment,' if I find myself getting very frustrated again, I will offer to invite my in-laws over for Thanksgiving. However, if I can manage my frustrating feelings, I will go buy that sweater I have been admiring, but have been reluctant to buy!"

SUMMARY

The ABC model can be a very effective way to manage self-defeating feelings. It provides a process for examining and disputing the cause(s) of emotional and behavioral problems that limit one's opportunity for positive mental health. It involves analyzing our perceptions about the events that contribute to our unhappiness. In the above case studies, both Frank and Susan demonstrate how they can manage their negative feelings so that their *goals* can be met. They did not "give in" to the negative events, nor did they passively accept them. Instead, by examining the reality of their situations, they were able to temper their harmful feelings. This process requires hard work and diligence . . . It is not magical.

8

Parents and Families of Children and Youth with Autism—Strategies for Support, Management, and Involvement

P rofessionals, along with parents and families, are increasingly recognizing the benefits of supporting parents and other family members of children and youth with autism. Two major reasons explain this change. First, all elements of a family are interconnected. Accordingly, events and circumstances that affect one family member will affect other members as well. Thus, a child or youth with autism will influence and be influenced by the entire family, necessitating that parents, families, and professionals focus their attention on more than just the child with autism. Failure to consider parent and family needs may result in overinvolvement by parents and family members with their child with autism (i.e., other family members needs are overlooked as a result of excessive attempts to satisfy an autistic child's needs), parent and family frustration, and/or poor communication between professionals and families. With more and more individuals with autism residing at home, as opposed to residential and institutional environments, these considerations are increasingly taking on importance.

A second major reason for involvement with and support of parents and families of children and youth with autism relates to the extensive training and intervention needs most of these children present. As noted throughout this book, individuals with autism have significant needs in a variety of areas, including social, language, medical, behavioral, cognitive. As a result, professionals are often unable to satisfactorily meet autistic children's needs without assistance from parents and family members. Such assistance, in the form of effective parent-professional communication and use of home-based management and training programs, has proven to be an effective way to assist children and youth with autism. Thus, to the extent they are interested and able, parents and families should be involved in training, education, and treatment programs.

In this chapter, we discuss support measures and programs available to parents and families of children and youth with autism in an effort to assist parents in working with their children in home settings and in better advocating for them. Chapter 8 also identifies ways in which parents and families can become involved in the education and treatment of family members with autism. As a result, the emphasis is on understanding and working with educational and training programs, although other aspects of support are also discussed.

What types of support programs are needed by parents and families of children and youth with autism?

Families of children with autism differ widely; thus, their support and other needs vary. As a result, professionals must be able to individualize services and programs for parents and families, just as they do for children. Despite such diversity, however, most parent and family needs fall in five major categories: (a) education, training, and other programs for a family member with autism; (b) information exchange opportunities; (c) advocacy, legal/legislative, and partnership training; (d) home program application; and (e) counseling and support services.

What does education, training, intervention services and other programs for a family member with autism involve?

We are referring here to the need that virtually every parent and family has for appropriate services for the member of their family diagnosed with autism. That is, parents and families want to know that the autistic family member is receiving appropriate educational, training, medical, vocational, or other types of services—whether through a public school, state-supported program, or private facility. No other need is as basic as this; therefore, until this need is met other parental and family needs will be secondary.

What is involved in information exchange programs between parents/families and professionals?

Included here is parents' and family members' need for information as well as professionals' need for accurate and ongoing information from parents and families. Through such two-way communication, professionals must obtain relevant facts about children and families (e.g., developmental history, school history, family expectations) and, in turn, provide appropriate information, including progress reports, to parents and families.

Information to parents and family members should include assessment results while also allowing individuals a chance to discuss the findings. Even though parents and families may have received an interpretation of autism following an assessment of their child, many would benefit from a review of this information and from discussing issues associated with the disability and subsequent recommendations.

Parents and families should also receive a description of the educational, training, vocational, medical, therapeutic, or other program to be provided their child, including the training methods, behavioral remediation, and other therapeutic and intervention programs scheduled.

What is involved in advocacy, legal/legislative, and partnership training for parents and families?

Parents are the primary case managers for their children, and are ultimately responsible for their well being. Yet, even though parents have been granted significant authority in determining the programs, procedures, and treatments to be used with their disabled children, including those with autism, few provisions have been made for training parents in how to serve in this case manager role. Thus, in spite of being able to participate in school conferences and other parent-professional meetings and to work cooperatively with professionals, parents have not been trained in how to do so effectively. Accordingly, if parents and family members are expected to be able to function at a level consistent with their case manager role and assigned rights, they must be provided appropriate training.

This area of training includes several elements. First, parents and family members should receive information about how to participate in conferences and meetings and the rights and responsibilities of parents and families of children with autism. Second, they should be informed about how they can serve as advocates and case managers for disabled children and act as effective consumers of community, school, and agency services and resources. Although it cannot be assumed that all parents and families need or desire partnership, case manager, or advocacy training, many families of children with autism will make use of such preparation if offered.

What are the needs of parents and families of children and youth with autism as they relate to home program application and how can professionals help in satisfying these needs?

Both as tutors and behavior managers, parents and family members of children and youth with autism have proven valuable by extending professional intervention programs beyond classroom and clinic settings. For example, under professional direction, parents and family members can be trained to implement individualized tutoring and training programs with their own child. Such tutoring serves both to involve these individuals in their child's school or vocational program and to positively structure interactions between the family and child.

Parents and families have also been trained to employ behavior management and training procedures with children and youth with autism. This has allowed parents and families to effect planned behavior changes in the home and, thus, to extend the therapeutic influence of professionals.

Although some parents and families may be unmotivated or unsuited for this role, others are highly appropriate. Training of parents and families to serve in this capacity provides a vehicle for extending problem-solving efforts into nonprofessional environments and for coordinating parents' motivation for involvement, participation, and case management. Accordingly, professionals should be willing (and able) to train parents and family members so that they can work with children and youth with autism at home.

What are the counseling and support-service needs of parents and families of children and youth with autism and how can professionals help meet these needs?

A small percentage of parents and families of children with autism will need in-depth counseling and therapy. However, many others can benefit from participating in support groups. Such groups are designed to help families discuss and accommodate disabled members, including those with autism; provide useful information about persons with disabilities; and give nondisabled family members a chance to discuss issues related to living with a disabled individual. Support groups may be sponsored by schools, mental health agencies, or organizations such as The Autism Society of America (specific support resources are listed in the Appendix).

Professionals should be able to provide interested parents and family members information about support groups; in turn, parents and families must be able to correctly identify their support-group needs. While not every family will want or use them, support groups can be extremely valuable in assisting individuals to successfully live with and support family members with autism.

Should all parents and families of children and youth with autism be equally involved with their offspring and the professionals who serve them?

Parent and family needs vary and must, therefore, be planned for individually. Professionals should not assume that every parent and family member of a child with autism will have the same needs; and every family should not be expected to follow a rigid plan of involvement. Parents and families not only have different needs relative to children and youth with autism, but they are unique in terms of time, resources, motivation, skills, commitment, and interests. For example, while some parents and family members wish to interact and communicate with professionals frequently, others may prefer to be actively involved as advocates for a family member with autism; others may want to serve as home tutors and behavior managers; and still others may have relatively little interest in training their child with autism at home.

It is important that parents and family members have an opportunity to select, through discussions with professionals, the level of involvement and participation that fits their needs, style, and interests. Thus, parents and family members must not feel guilty if their level of participation and involvement differs from that of other parents and families. Further, professionals must respect these decisions and assist parents and family members in implementing programs that correspond to their participation and involvement interests and abilities.

It is also important that both families and professionals recognize that involvement and participation levels do not remain constant, but depend on parent and family circumstances at a given time. For example, a parent who actively serves as a home tutor for a child with autism may need to reduce her level of involvement after a divorce or the death of a spouse. Thus, parents, family members, and professionals must be flexible and willing to vary their support of a family member with autism according to family circumstances. The underlying consideration is that family members must be able to identify and satisfy their own needs in order to successfully support a family member with autism.

A great deal has been said and written about parent and family involvement. Just how important is parent and family involvement relative to children and youth with autism?

There is no question that children and adolescents, including those with autism, are greatly influenced by their parents and families. In fact, no other single experience impacts so profoundly on the way we react to the world and its people. Our values, attitudes, and unique ways of behaving are often a direct result of parent and family influence. This is not to suggest that children and adolescents with autism do not develop behaviors that are uniquely their own; or that they will not be influenced by others, such as peers, teachers, language pathologists, and so on. Nonetheless, parents and families can be involved in problem solving, training, and support activities. In fact, parent and family support is necessary for children's optimal growth and development. The role of parents and families in this area may include acting as (a) referral agents, (b) support agents, and (c) case managers for their children. As noted earlier, the degree of parent and family involvement will vary; however, it is important to recognize the influential role parents and family members can play in the lives of children and youth with autism.

What is involved in parents and families acting as a referral agent?

Parents occasionally find that the professionals they respect the most and have the most contact with do not share their concern over their children's behavior. In response to a parent's concern about her child's behavior, a pediatrician or a family physician, for example, may suggest that the child is going through a phase or that a given concern is unfounded. One mother observed that every time she attempted to talk to her family doctor about her son's problems, the doctor wanted to write her a prescription for tranquilizers. In spite of exceptions to this pattern, many parents find it difficult to find suitable professional help for their children.

Parents can take a number of steps to ensure that pediatricians, other physicians, and other professionals with whom they have contact (e.g., public health nurses, social workers) note their concerns. First, make it clear that you are not asking the doctor (or other professional) to personally solve the problem. Explain that you are concerned about your child's behavior and are seeking an assessment by a professional trained and experienced in working with children and adolescents with disabilities, including autism. Physicians and other professionals sometimes lack the time and expertise to deal with children with developmental delays and problems. Therefore, it is important to emphasize that you are not asking the individual to solve the problem on the spot.

Second, document your concerns. Rather than telling a professional from whom you are seeking assistance, "My child prefers to be by himself," attempt to identify precisely what it is your child is doing. For instance, does "prefers to be by himself" mean that he likes to play by himself in the same room as other family members?; that he actively avoids being near others?; or that he engages in self-stimulatory behaviors (e.g., hand flapping) to such an extent that he becomes unaware of the presence of others? Further, report how often, how intensely, and how long the problem occurs. Specifying that your child daily engages in self-stimulatory behavior for extended periods of time to the exclusion of all other activities and that this behavior has occurred consistently over the past year is far more meaningful than simply relating that your child rocks. Early intervention is particularly important for children with autism, making it essential to find appropriate assistance as soon as possible.

What should I do if my doctor doesn't share my concern?

Seek help for your child's behavior even if your doctor does not share your concern. If you have observed unusual behavior patterns over extended periods of time (e.g., extreme withdrawal for 1–2 months or more), seek outside professional help. The best source of referral information is your community or county mental health agency. You may also contact the Autism Society of America or your state's autism society. Your child's problem may turn out to be insignificant and temporary. However, if you consider it significant and if it is disruptive or bothersome to you and your family, contact an appropriate professional or agency.

Can referrals for service be made by and through public school personnel?

"Yes." While most children with autism are diagnosed prior to the time they begin school, they are occasionally identified during their elementary-school years. This is particularly true for students with high-functioning autism disorder.

School personnel may be the first professionals to contact parents regarding their concerns about a child. For instance, a kindergarten teacher may call a parent after having observed that a child has poor social skills or after noticing that he displays unusual behavior patterns. Contacts of this type are usually designed to elicit background information (e.g., developmental history, diagnostic information); to seek guidance regarding problem-solving strategies (e.g., parents' behavior management suggestions); and to obtain permission to conduct evaluations. Parents should be aware that public school personnel cannot evaluate children thought to be exceptional without first gaining written parental approval. Similarly, school personnel must obtain parental permission prior to placing a child in a special-education program.

Parents may also seek assistance from school personnel regarding their children's behavior and development. As in dealings with medical personnel, teacher contacts are most productive when concerns are specific and documented. Tell your child's teacher exactly what your concern is; how frequently and intensely the problem occurs; and how long it has been going on. Public schools are required to provide assessment and educational services for handicapped children and youth, including those with autism. Thus, you may secure an evaluation for your child at no cost to you. If it is agreed that your child has a problem that should be investigated, ask the teacher to initiate a referral for evaluation.

What if the teacher doesn't think my child has a problem?

If a teacher or other school professional (e.g., principal, counselor) does not agree that a problem exists, you may still request an evaluation. Such a request should be made if you have reason to believe a child has a serious problem. To request an evaluation, write the director of special education in your local school district. If you do not have the name and address, call the board of education or the school administration office in your city. Your letter should specify the basis for your concern, request a district evaluation, and be accompanied by copies of relevant background documents (e.g., evaluation reports, developmental charts). School districts are required by state and federal mandate to consider parental requests for evaluation.

What does it mean to be a "support agent"?

Children with autism seldom make significant improvement unless the meaningful individuals in their lives work together. Thus, parents cannot expect their child to significantly improve exclusively as a result of professionals' efforts. Rather, parents and professionals must work together. Although parents' role in this regard will vary, it can be expected to include cooperation and support for agreed-upon plans. In many instances, professionals develop plans for parents and families to follow. For example, parents may be asked to establish and maintain certain rules; take certain actions; or collect and/or provide certain types of information. For children to benefit the most, parents must support agreed-upon decisions and recommendations. Not only should parents and families be involved in decision making, once a decision has been reached, they must also support it.

What does being a "case manager" mean?

A case manager advocates for and represents or acts in support of another. In the case of parents of children and youth with autism, this means that children's interests receive priority and that parents and family members take responsibility for ensuring that the various needs of a family member with a disability are met. Although this may lead parents to view their situation differently from professionals, it does not mean that parents should disagree with, distrust, or otherwise resist cooperating with professionals. Conversely, parents should not unthinkingly accept all recommendations and suggestions without considering child and family needs as well as alternative recommendations. Parents and professionals must strive for a partnership in which both parties have the right to voice their opinions and to disagree. Such an open relationship strengthens the partnership and ultimately improves services to children.

The parents of a 16-year-old youth with autism found themselves caught between loyalty to their local school district and their son's interests. The school district had historically been responsive to their child's needs, including starting an elementary program for students with autism. When the boy outgrew the elementary program, however, the district did not have a suitable alternative available. Instead, school personnel recommended that the boy be placed in a high-school learning disability program since that was the only service available. The parents found themselves in the uncomfortable position of wanting to support the school district, but knowing that the recommended service was not in their son's best interest. Open discussion of concerns between school staff and parents led the district to contract for appropriate services from a neighboring district. Only by taking case-management responsibility and advocating for their son were these parents able to secure a suitable program.

Can parents be effective case managers and advocates for their children and still cooperate with professionals?

Parents, including those of children and youth with autism, must seek to cooperate with and trust professionals. However, cooperation and trust do not mean passive compliance with suggestions and strategies that may not be in a child's best interests; nor an expectation that others will take total responsibility for meeting a child's needs. Thus, parents must trust and support the professionals with whom they interact while keeping their child's interests a priority. Moreover, they should be willing to actively work to make sure their child's needs are being met.

Are there other things parents and families can do to advocate for a family member with autism?

Being an effective advocate and case manager for a child or youth with autism implies having available appropriate knowledge and information about persons with disabilities. In particular, parents and family members who expect to effectively represent or support a family member with autism must be familiar with legislation that relates to children with disabilities. Of particular significance in this regard is the Individuals with Disabilities Education Act (formerly the Education For All Handicapped Children's Act). Services for children and youth with autism involve more than education, yet this program component is so significant that it should receive priority consideration. In this regard, advocacy and case management functions will directly relate to the aforementioned legislation.

What is the Individuals with Disabilities Education Act, and how can knowledge about this enactment help parents and families advocate for a family member with autism?

The most comprehensive and significant legislation yet proposed and enacted for meeting the needs of school-age handicapped children and youth (including those with autism) has been the Education for All Handicapped Children Act of 1975. This law (amended and retitled the Individuals with Disabilities Education Act in 1990) is so significant and far reaching that it dominates every prior piece of legislation enacted for children and youth with disabilities. In 1986, P.L. 99-457 extended the requirements of P.L. 94-142 to children aged 3 to 5, thus further expanding the significance of this monumental legislation. The impact of P.L. 94-142 is complemented and expanded by Section 504 of the Rehabilitation Act of 1975. Although both laws share a similar purpose, that is, to promote the rights of persons with disabilities, Section 504 of the Rehabilitation Act of 1975 broadens the range of individuals affected by expanding the age and definition requirements.

The Education for All Handicapped Children Act of 1975 was designed to ensure a free and appropriate public education for all handicapped children and youth. This law, signed into effect by President Gerald Ford on November 29, 1975, after nearly four years of legislative proceedings, provides guidelines for aiding states and individual agencies (including public schools) in offering suitable educational experiences to children and youth with disabilities and in ensuring that the rights of these individuals and their families are protected. Many of the specific procedures involved in P.L. 94-142 are contained in individual "state plans"—documents that explain the precise manner in which each state will provide educational provisions and alternatives for children and youth with disabilities, including those identified as having autism.

Specific elements of the Act include the following:

1. Nondiscriminatory assessment in diagnosis.

2. The right to due process, which protects exceptional children and youth from erroneous classification and denial of equal education and protection.

3. Placement of disabled students in an appropriate educational setting, that is, the least restrictive environment.

4. Individualized program plans, which ensure an appropriate education.

5. Involvement of parents in their children's education.

What is meant by the "nondiscriminatory assessment in diagnosis" component of the Individuals with Disabilities Education Act?

The Individuals with Disabilities Education Act requires that testing and evaluation methods used to diagnose students with disabilities (including those with autism) not be racially or culturally discriminatory. Moreover, the evaluation procedures must accommodate a student's native language. Thus, non-English-speaking children being evaluated because of an alleged school problem must be tested using materials and procedures that allow them to use their native language. Further, the evaluation process must be designed to accommodate students' deficits. For instance, a student with limited spoken language must not be evaluated by means of tests that require extensive verbal responses.

According to the law, parents (or legal custodians) have a right to be actively involved in the assessment process. Thus, parents of children being recommended for evaluation due to a school problem or an alleged disability must give written permission prior to any evaluations.

Requests for evaluation can be made not only by schools but also by parents. Hence, parents of a child exhibiting autistic-like characteristics can request an evaluation or reevaluation of their offspring at any time. However, a school district has the choice of conducting or refusing to conduct an evaluation. In the event the district agrees to an evaluation, they must still obtain written parental permission. If, on the other hand, the district takes the position that an evaluation is not needed, they must notify the parents, in writing, of their decision. This notice must also inform the parents that, if they desire, they can request a hearing to arbitrate differences of opinion between the school and themselves regarding the need for an evaluation.

As discussed in Chapter 3, evaluations of children and youth considered to have autism or other disabilities should be both *multidisciplinary* and *comprehensive*. Consequently, evaluations must encompass information relating to physical, psychological, sociological, and educational status. Furthermore, they must be conducted by a variety of "experts" representing different fields, as opposed to a single individual. Thus, evaluations primarily conducted by school personnel may involve professionals other than school employees. For example, in instances where a child with autism requires an evaluation by a professional who is not on a school's staff (e.g., audiologist, neurologist), a school would be required to privately contract for those diagnostic services.

What does the "right to due process" component of the Individuals with Disabilities Education Act refer to?

The primary due-process rights afforded parents and children under the act include parental access to records, independent evaluations, surrogate parents, parental notice, and right to a hearing. Each of these rights is identified below.

Parental access to records.   Parents or legal custodians are allowed to view all records pertaining to the identification, assessment, and placement of their child.

Independent evaluations.   Parents and legal custodians are entitled to obtain an evaluation of their son or daughter from qualified (licensed or certified) examiners not affiliated with the district or agency recommending the action. However, even though parents are entitled to seek their own independent evaluation and even though schools or agencies may be required to recommend appropriate individuals to conduct the evaluation, parents may be required to assume the costs of such an evaluation.

Appointment of surrogate parents.   In instances where a child or adolescent is a ward of the state, or the parents are unavailable or unknown, a surrogate parent must be appointed. Surrogate parents are commissioned to represent the child in all matters pertaining to evaluation, placement, and education. The criteria for selection of a surrogate parent stipulate that the appointee have the necessary competence to represent an exceptional child or adolescent (including an individual with autism) and that no conflict of interest exist. Thus, individuals employed by or affiliated with an institution or setting in which a child or adolescent is a resident should not serve as surrogate parents.

Right to parental notice.   As discussed earlier, parents, legal custodians, or surrogates must be provided written notice whenever a school or agency proposes to conduct an evaluation or make a change in the educational program for an exceptional pupil, including a child or youth identified as having autism. This requirement also applies in instances where parents request changes or evaluations.

Right to hearing.   Parents and legal custodians must be provided a formal opportunity to present complaints on any matter relating to the identification, evaluation, or educational placement of their child. This process is designed to offer parents, schools, and agencies an objective and impartial hearing, the outcome of which is intended to lead to the most appropriate educational placement possible for a child. Hearings can be held by the state, intermediate, or local educational agency, depending on the situation and locale.

The provisions of due process are not only extended to parents and legal custodians but also to agencies and schools. Thus, a school or agency is entitled to a hearing on its recommendation to initiate or refuse evaluation or placement procedures.

It is important that parents and family members of children and youth with autism recognize their due-process rights under the Individuals with Disabilities Education Act. Without this information it is impossible to act as an effective advocate and case manager. However, availability of this information must not be viewed as an alternative to directly communicating and working with professionals. As noted before, children and youth with autism make the best progress when parents/family members and professionals work jointly; and when parents and family members are actively involved in identifying and managing services.

What does the Individuals with Disabilities Education Act provision of "placement in the least restrictive environment" refer to?

According to this provision, school-age disabled children and youth, including those with autism, must be educated with nondisabled students to the maximum extent appropriate. Disabled children and youth can be placed outside the regular classroom only when the severity or nature of their handicap demands a more restrictive setting.

While the regulations pertaining to the least restrictive environment advocate the regular classroom as the desired location for instruction, this policy does not apply to children and youth whose needs cannot be adequately met in that setting. Thus, children and youth with autism who require special education or a more restrictive setting (e.g., hospital or residential program) are assured of such a program. The identification of the least restrictive environment, which is reviewed and determined at least annually, must be based on each child or youth's ability and performance, as translated through the Individualized Education Program (IEP). Since parents or legal custodians are major participants in this decision, this decision cannot be made by school or agency personnel without family input.

What is an "Individualized Education Program" (IEP)?

An Individualized Education Program (IEP) must be provided for each child or adolescent identified as needing special education, including children and youth with autism. An IEP is a written statement outlining the manner in which each disabled child's unique needs will be met. Thus, each IEP is different. The document is developed in a meeting attended by professionals, parents and, when appropriate, the child or youth.

For each child, the IEP includes the following:

(a) A statement of child's strengths, weaknesses, and functioning level (e.g., language, social skill, behavior, cognitive, self-help abilities);

(b) annual goals, or statements of areas in which professionals will focus their attention (e.g., to improve self-help skills, to improve social interaction skills);

(c) short-term objectives, statements identifying the specifics of annual goals (e.g., James will initiate at least one appropriate social greeting, as defined by his teacher, with a peer on the school playground, on 5 consecutive days);

(d) a statement of the specific educational services to be provided (e.g., speech pathology, occupational therapy);

(e) the extent to which a student will be able to participate in regular educational programs (e.g., James will be scheduled for lunch in the cafeteria at the same time as his same-age peers);

(f) projected dates for initiation and duration of services (e.g., James will be scheduled for individual occupational therapy 30 minutes two times per week between September 1 and May 15);

(g) objective criteria for determining whether objectives are being achieved (James will achieve 80 % accuracy, as judged by his teacher, on a 20-minute, three-part vocational collating task for five consecutive days).

According to the Individuals with Disabilities Education Act, the IEP must be written or revised each school year. Although the IEP format can vary among states, school districts, and agencies (e.g., residential treatment programs for children with autism), the basic components previously outlined, must always be included. The IEP is not intended to serve as a legally binding contract whereby districts, hospitals, residential centers, and agencies are bound to demonstrate that progress specified in the annual goals and objectives has been met. However, professionals must use appropriate methods to achieve specified goals and objectives, including those stated in the IEP.

Individuals who should be involved in the IEP conference include a representative of the school, hospital, residential center, or agency providing the services (other than the teacher); the teacher(s) who will implement the IEP; the parent(s) or legal custodians; the child/youth, when appropriate; and others, at the discretion of the parents or program. During the development of the initial IEP, the district or agency recommending the program modification should also have available someone who can interpret testing and diagnostic procedures to parents.

Because parents are considered to play such an integral role in the IEP conference, and because effective case management requires parent and family involvement, provisions exist for guaranteeing parental participation. Specifically, parents must receive advance notice of the IEP conference, including the purpose, time, location, and those individuals who will attend. Further, the conferences must be held at times and places mutually convenient to the parents and professionals. Those individuals coordinating the conference must also ensure that parents are able to comprehend and offer input into the session (e.g., interpreters must be provided for deaf or non-English-speaking parents); in the event that parents are unable to attend the session, the school, program, or agency must use other methods to allow parental participation (e.g., conference telephone calls). Although IEP conferences can be held without parental representation, the district or agency is required to document that parents were provided an opportunity to participate.

What is meant by the Individuals with Disabilities Education Act's provision of "involvement of parents in their children's education"?

The act guarantees not only the right to a free and appropriate education for all children with handicaps, including those with autism, but also the involvement of parents in decision-making, educational planning, and implementation. That is, parents are clearly afforded opportunities to be case managers for their children. This policy represents a radical departure from past practices whereby parents and families were often blamed for conditions such as autism and isolated from professional decision-making. In contrast, the Individuals with Disabilities Education Act allows and encourages parent involvement and case-management opportunities in educational and related service matters that affect their children. As previously discussed, parental rights include: being a part of the process for assessing their child; challenging their child's evaluation, program, or placement recommendations; giving or withholding evaluation or placement consent; having access to records; and planning their child's education and treatment program.

Obviously, mandated parent involvement is not sufficient to establish and maintain a productive professional-family relationship. Yet, the Individuals with Disabilities Education Act clearly provides a legislative structure for meaningful involvement of parents, families, and professionals. To be effective, family advocacy and case management on behalf of children and youth with autism require familiarity with this law.

What else can parents and families do to help family members who have been diagnosed with autism?

Parents and family members often experience difficulty in managing the behavior of children and youth with autism. Since success in this area is often basic to children's improvement as well as family tranquility, rule setting and behavior management are areas in which parents and family members may make a valuable contribution.

What can parents and family members do to set good rules?

Knowing limits and expectations is necessary and beneficial for all children and youth, but particularly so for individuals with autism who often have difficulty establishing their own structure. Steps involved in setting and implementing effective rules are identified below.

1. **Rules should be purposeful.** For instance, a rule may state that a child will not play in the street *because it is dangerous;* or that a child will not play in the toilet *because it is unhygienic and socially unacceptable.* Thus, each rule should accomplish a specific goal, usually to protect a child or to maintain order. Such clarity requires that both a *specific* target behavior (e.g., complying with parent requests, as

opposed to "not minding") and a *specific* consequence (loss of bicycle privileges for 24 hours, as opposed to "something you will regret") be identified. Rules should also specify rewards for following rules as opposed to negative consequences for noncompliance. It is also important that rules be designed not simply to demonstrate control. Telling a child she cannot do certain things merely to show that you are in charge and can control her behavior is unacceptable. Additionally, children must not be expected to do things they cannot understand or perform. For example, it is unrealistic to expect a nonverbal autistic child to talk in complete sentences before he is allowed to eat.

2. **Attempt to involve children.** Children tend to be more accepting of rules they have helped develop. Although the extent of such involvement will vary with children's age and ability, many children, including those with autism, can be involved. In some cases, parents may simply explain why a rule is being implemented (e.g., "You cannot play in the street because you might get hurt"). Other situations require more discussion. Thus, a teenager with high-functioning autism disorder may be actively involved in rule-setting discussions with his parents.

3. **Limit the number of rules.** "The fewer the better" is a good guideline for rule setting. Long lists of rules are not only difficult to remember, they also tend to become meaningless and be taken less seriously.

4. **Establish fair and appropriate consequences.** Children must understand precisely what will happen if they comply or fail to comply with certain rules (e.g., "If you refrain from hitting at dinner you may go for a drive with dad."). Only when such understanding is assured can consequences be effectively applied. Additionally, parents must make sure that consequences are reasonable and enforceable. They must not be too easy or too severe. Similarly, impulsive and unenforceable consequences must be avoided (e.g., "You must stay in your room the rest of the day"). Also, parents must be able to enforce established rules. For example, do not tell an adolescent with autism that he must interact with peers in the neighborhood when you have no means of enforcing such a rule.

5. **Be consistent.** A consequence must occur *every* time a rule condition is met. As a result, adults and/or family members must be willing to apply the consequence any time the target behavior occurs, even if it happens at a highly inopportune time. Additionally, in applying consequences parents should attempt to adhere to the following guidelines: (a) do not argue and negotiate—when a rule infraction occurs, apply the stated consequence with a minimum of explanation and without

allowing an argument to develop; (b) avoid emotional displays when applying the consequence—do what you said you would do in a straightforward, businesslike manner (demonstrating to children that you are hurt or upset has little positive effect); (c) apply the consequence after rule conditions have been met—never before. Telling a child, for example, that you have decided to provide him an agreed-upon trip prior to his meeting the conditions for the trip often has a negative effect on the overall behavior management program.

6. **Use positive as well as negative consequences.** It is not unusual for parents (and children!) to think of rules exclusively in negative terms. For example, families may think only in terms of what a child will lose if he or she violates a rule. However, rules tend to work best when rewards (including praise and attention) are used. If negative consequences are applied, they should be used along with positive consequences (e.g., reward for following a rule).

Are there other things I can do to manage my child's behavior?

"Yes." *Follow routine schedules.* Children and adolescents with autism tend to be positively influenced by structure and routines. For example, set bedtimes and meal times often aid children in understanding and following schedules and parental requests. Conversely, problems may occur when children are unable to anticipate events and activities. This does not mean that parents and families must never vary their schedules—such a practice is neither realistic nor desirable. However, basic schedules and routines have been found to reduce management problems.

Another effective management tool is to *plan activities for children.* This does not mean that something must be scheduled for every waking minute—this would not only be burdensome for parents but a problem for children. However, behavioral problems are most apt to occur during unstructured times. Thus, parents may outline for their offspring which activities are available to them after school and on weekends (e.g., puzzle work, ball playing, bicycling, summer camp). Parents will probably discover that the more involved children become in structured and productive activities, the less likely they are to engage in deviant acts.

Are there management programs designed to increase or decrease specific behaviors?

Rules and other general management techniques may fail to change some behaviors. In such situations, more structured management techniques may be necessary. Although parents are usually able to successfully use behavior-change methods, these stricter procedures should be set up and followed by a trained professional, preferably someone who is familiar in working with children and youth with autism.

What are the steps in a behavior-management program?

As noted in Chapter 6, setting up and carrying out behavior-management programs with children with autism should follow a series of basic steps and principles. Because of their importance, these steps are discussed below, specifically as applied by parents and family members.

Step 1: Identify a specific behavior to be increased or decreased.   Behavior management programs work best when applied to well-defined behaviors. For example, attempting to change a behavior such as "hyperactivity" or "social immaturity" is difficult because the target behavior may differ in the eyes of various people, including the child. For example, one parent might define "social immaturity" as failing to follow parental directions while another may view it as avoiding peers. As a result, parents wishing to change a behavior must specifically define it.

What is involved in "specifically defining a behavior"?

Definitions are most effective when they specify the *what* (what the behavior is), *where* (where the behavior will be observed and dealt with), and *when* (when the behavior will be observed and dealt with) of a behavior.

- The *what* requires that parents precisely define a behavior. For example, *hitting* might be defined as a child making contact with another person with his fist, hand, or arm. This definition makes no attempt to differentiate between soft and hard hits, or purposeful or accidental hitting. A hit is a hit!

- The *where* identifies settings, specifically those where the target behavior will be observed and dealt with. For example, a program for hitting might be applied at home or at the babysitter's, but not at the store; particularly, if it is impossible to carry out the consequence in a store setting.

- The *when* part of the definition specifies the times during which the program will be applied (e.g., 7:00–8:30 pm Monday–Friday).

Are there other definition issues I should consider when attempting to change my child's behavior?

"Yes." Make sure that the behavior you wish to change is under the child's control; otherwise, it cannot be changed through this management system. Behaviors such as slamming a door, saying "thank you," and throwing rocks at the family cat are ordinarily under a child's control. In contrast, seizures, tremors, and tics are examples of behaviors that are generally not under an individual's control and, thus, usually not subject to change using these techniques.

What are the other steps in setting up a behavior-management program?

Step 2: Determine the settings and situations surrounding the problem.
This simply means that you should examine the conditions associated with the problem. Does the behavior only occur around certain people (e.g., mother, babysitter) or at certain times (e.g., dinner, bedtime)? Identifying these factors is helpful. For example, if it can be determined that a child has a certain problem only with his father, the solution may involve improving their relationship rather than developing a formal management program.

Step 3: Evaluate what you do when the behavior occurs and what you have done in the past to change it.
In dealing with their autistic children's behavior, parents and families resort to a number of methods, some of which are more successful than others. For example, children may be talked to, spanked, put in time-out, given food for following rules, and so forth. Knowing what options have been used in the past is a basic step in planning for the future. In addition, try to understand your own and other family members' reactions to a given problem (see Chapter 7 for a detailed

discussion of this concept). For instance, one mother who was extremely concerned about her daughter's reluctance to play with other children realized that her response to this problem might be maintaining it. Thus, she observed that when her child came home from school, she immediately began nagging her to go outside and play with neighborhood children. Apparently, the child enjoyed her mother's attention, even though it was negative, because when the mother ceased nagging, the child became more interested in playing with other children.

Step 4: Select and apply suitable consequences.   After defining a behavior and the circumstances surrounding it, apply appropriate methods for changing it. The length of time interventions should be applied will vary from situation to situation and from child to child; however, it is important to apply the chosen methods long enough for them to have a chance to work. Parents should not change programs without first consulting the professional responsible for setting up the program.

Four major types of consequences may be used by parents and family members to change behavior: positive consequences, ignoring, negative consequences, and environmental changes.

Step 5: Evaluate the effectiveness of your management methods.   The effectiveness of behavior-management consequences and methods will vary depending on specific children and conditions. Thus, a technique may work with some children with autism and not with others. Therefore, it is essential to evaluate a program. Without such evaluation parents may continue to use ineffective methods or drop an effective procedure.

What are "positive consequences" and how are they used?

As noted in Chapter 6, *positive consequences* are events that increase a behavior. They come in two major forms: *contingent activities* and *social consequences.* Contingent activities, also known as "Grandma's law," make preferred activities dependent upon desired behavior. For example, children or adolescents may be told, "When you finish your homework you may watch TV"; "You may ride your bicycle after you take out the trash"; or "If you avoid hitting your brothers and sisters this afternoon, you may go to Dairy King with your brother." As illustrated, a desired activity is used to encourage a specific, desirable behavior.

Social consequences include praise, parental attention, smiles, and hugs for desired behavior. When used consistently, these forms of human contact and appreciation are powerful motivators. Thus, parents may recognize their children for specific deeds (e.g., "I appreciate your following directions"), realizing that when such attention consistently follows a desired behavior, the behavior will often be repeated.

How is ignoring used as a behavior-management technique?

Ignoring may decrease problem behaviors that occur as a result of attention. For instance, a child who tantrums to make her parents give in to her demands may cease this behavior if family members ignore her when she begins to cry.

When attempting to change a behavior through ignoring, consider the following: (a) At first, ignoring may increase the target behavior. That is, children may initially try to gain attention by increasing the problem behavior; (b) Ignoring works only if everyone involved is able to ignore. In instances where children are ignored only some of the time and by some people, the system usually fails.

It is also extremely important to keep in mind that in order to decrease a behavior through ignoring you must give attention for acceptable behavior. Thus, you must ignore behavior you want to decrease while paying attention to behavior you want to increase. If you fail to give attention for suitable behavior, you probably will not be able to decrease a negative behavior through ignoring.

What are negative consequences and how are they used to change behavior?

Negative consequences or punishment (see Chapter 6 for additional discussion) refer to undesirable events that follow specific behaviors. For example, children may learn that they will lose privileges (e.g., watching a favorite videotape) if they do certain things.

What kinds of negative consequences are available for use by parents and families?

A number of negative consequences are available, one of which is *time-out*. Time-out involves placing a child in a chair in a corner (or similar spot) when he or she displays a certain unacceptable behavior. For example, a child may be required to sit quietly for 3 minutes in a chair in the corner of the living room if he throws things around the house. When used correctly, this popular consequence often leads to positive results.

Time-out is most effective if used with specific behaviors. Timing kids out for a variety of unacceptable behaviors usually reduces the potential effectiveness of this management tool. Additionally, the time-out site should be clear of toys, TV, and other interesting things, including people. Thus, parents and family members must ignore children in time-out. Further, time-out sessions should be short: 3–5 minutes of quiet have proven best. If children are crying at the end of the specified time, time-out should be extended until the crying stops. Finally, parents or others using time-out should limit their comments to the child (e.g., "No kicking; go to time out.") until the time-out period is over.

As with other management options, time-out may not work with every child with autism. Indeed, some children prefer being by themselves in time-out. Under such circumstances, time-out obviously does not decrease the behavior for which it was intended, hence alternative interventions must be identified.

What does "changing the environment" mean and how is it used as a management method?

Changing the environment may take a variety of forms, including any change in conditions that may be causing problems. For example, one child with autism threw severe tantrums whenever a mealtime routine was broken. Since this was the only circumstance that provoked a tantrum, the parents tried consistently to follow established mealtimes. They also found that telling their child, well in advance, that there would be a change reduced the chances of a tantrum. Another parent of a preschool child diagnosed with autism solved her child's problem of throwing decorative glass objects (no other types of items were thrown) by moving these objects out of the child's reach. As suggested by these examples, simple methods are often sufficient for dealing with problems.

With regard to setting up a behavior-management program, what does evaluation involve?

Evaluation ordinarily requires daily monitoring of a target behavior. Parents are advised to seek the help of a psychologist or other qualified mental-health worker or educator when developing evaluation methods.

Are there things parents can do to make sure programs work?

Behavior-management programs do not work 100% of the time. However, the best results occur when the following basic steps are followed:

1. Apply a consequence only *after* a target behavior. Do not allow a child to engage in a desired activity because you have faith he will complete an agreed-upon chore, for example. Rather, wait until he completes the chore. Similarly, do not apply a negative consequence (e.g., place a child in time-out) because she *looked* like she was going to engage in some undesirable activity.

2. Apply the consequence *consistently.* Carry out whatever you said you would do each time the behavior occurs.

3. Apply the consequence as soon after the target behavior occurs as possible. Waiting diminishes the strength of the consequence.

4. Make a commitment to apply a procedure over time. Behavior management programs sometimes work quickly—at other times, it takes a while. However, unless they are used consistently for a significant length of time, they will probably not be successful. Thus, do not stop using a program when it starts to work. It is sometimes tempting to drop a procedure when the target behavior improves, but most programs stop being effective when we stop working to apply them!

5. Seek professional guidance when setting up a behavior-management program. Once a program has been decided upon, it is important that you follow the plan and not make changes in what was agreed upon.

Is there more to dealing with a child with autism than using rules and management techniques?

Dealing satisfactorily with a child or adolescent who has autism requires more than sound rules and management techniques. Parents and family members must be able to establish a relationship with their offspring. Moreover, as discussed in Chapter 7, the attitudes of parents and family members are extremely important.

How do I go about establishing a relationship with my child who has autism?

Just as with normally developing children and youth, children with autism need positive relationships with their families. That is, parents and family members must not simply be dispensers of reinforcers or serve as tutors, social-skill trainers, language developers, or advocates without also developing positive, interpersonal relationships with their children. It is extremely important, therefore, that parents and family members set aside time to be with their child with autism. Such involvement is as much a part of being an effective case manager as making sure that a child is receiving all necessary services.

Developing a relationship takes time and effort. Thus, parents must spend time with their children doing mutually enjoyable things. In addition to peer tutoring, training, and similar activities, parents and family members must engage in games and leisure pursuits with their children. Moreover, as much as possible, family members with autism should be included in family outings and events (e.g., going shopping, going to sports events), for social and learning reasons. In some instances, children with autism need to be prompted to engage in such activities (e.g., walking with a parent after dinner, looking at a book with a brother or sister, going grocery shopping); however, the trust, rapport, and experiences acquired through such activities often facilitate growth and development; enhance children's response to management and skill-development programs; develop social, cognitive, and independent living skills; and establish more normalized family relationships. Chapter 7 provides additional information in this regard.

SUMMARY

Parents and other family members play a prominent role in the growth and development of their children with autism. They are the primary case managers for their children. They serve as referral agents, advocates, and behavior managers. To adequately fulfill all these roles, parents must seek appropriate professional services; establish fair, yet firm rules; and use appropriate management techniques to deal with specific problems. The degree of success with which these roles are fulfilled will almost always influence the growth and development of children and youth with autism.

REFERENCES

American Psychiatric Association (1987). *Diagnostic and statistical manual of mental disorders* (3rd ed., rev.). Washington, DC: Author.

American Psychiatric Association (1980). *Diagnostic and statistical manual of mental disorders* (3rd ed.). Washington, DC: Author.

Bayley, N. (1969). *Bayley scales of infant development.* New York: Psychological Corporation.

Bettelheim, B. (1967). *The empty fortress.* New York: Free Press.

Grandin, T. (1988). Teaching tips from a recovered autistic. *Focus on Autistic Behavior, 3*(1), 1–8.

Kanner, L. (1943). Autistic disturbances of affective contact. *Nervous Child, 2,* 217–250.

Krug, D., Arick, J., & Almond, P. (1980). *Autism screening instrument for educational planning.* Austin, TX: PRO-ED.

Leiter, R. G. (1948). *The Leiter international performance scale.* Chicago: Stoelting.

McCarthy, D. (1972). *McCarthy scales of children's abilities.* New York: Psychological Corporation.

Rendle-Short, J. (1978). *Infantile autism diagnosis.* Washington, DC: National Society for Autistic Children.

Simpson, R., & Regan, M. (1986). *Management of autistic behavior.* Austin, TX: PRO-ED.

Thorndike, R. L., Hagen E. P., & Saettler, J. M. (1986). *Standord-Binet Intelligence Scale* (4th ed.). Chicago: Riverside Publishing.

APPENDIX A: CHAPTER QUESTIONS

3. Identification and Assessment of Children and Youth with Autism and Pervasive Developmental Disorders   33

5. Sources of Assistance for Children and Youth with Autism   **79**

6. Treatment and Interventions for Children and Youth with Autism   **95**

8. Parents and Families of Children and Youth with Autism— Strategies for Support, Management, and Involvement 137

APPENDIX B: RESOURCES

Organizations. In many states, local, state, and regional organizations, both parent and professional, serve as resources to parents. The most influential national organization is the Autism Society of America (ASA; formerly the National Society for Children, or NSAC). Services include information and referral, an advocate newsletter, a bookstore, an annual conference, and chapter services. ASA can also inform you of any state or local organizations near you.

Two other resources are the state Board of Education, Office of Special Education in your state, and the state chapter of the Council for Exceptional Children. To contact these service organizations, write:

Autism Society of America
8601 Georgia Ave.
Suite 503
Silver Springs, MD 20910

Council for Exceptional Children
1920 Association Drive
Reston, VA 22091-1589

Other organizations that may be of service include:

American Association for the Advancement of Behavior Therapy
305 E. Forty-fifth Street
New York, NY 10017

American Association of Mental Retardation
5101 Wisconsin Avenue NW
Washington, DC 20016

American Association of Psychiatric Clinics for Children
250 W. Fifty-Seventh Street
New York, NY 10019

American Association of Psychiatric Services for Children
1701 Eighteenth Street, NW
Washington, DC 20009

American Personnel and Guidance Association
5203 Leesburg Pike
Falls Church, VA 22041

American Printing House for the Blind
1839 Frankfort Avenue
Lousiville, KY 40206

American Psychological Association
1200 17th Street, NW
Washington, DC 20036

American Vocational Association
2020 North Fourteenth Street
Arlington, VA 22201

Association for Persons with Severe Handicaps
7010 Roosevelt Way NE
Seattle, WA 98115

Beach Center on Families and Disability
Bureau of Child Research
4138 Haworth Hall
University of Kansas
Lawrence, KS 60045

Center for Innovation in Teaching the Handicapped
Indiana University
2805 East Tenth St.
Bloomington, IN 47401

Child Welfare League of America
67 Irving Place
New York, NY 10003

Children's Defense Fund
1520 New Hampshire Avenue, NW
Washington, DC 20036

Closer Look—National Information Center for the Handicapped
1201 16th Street, NW
Washington, DC 20036

Co-Ordinating Council for Handicapped Children
407 South Dearborn, Room 400
Chicago, IL 60605

March of Dimes
1275 Mamaroneck Avenue
White Plains, NY 10605

National Association for the Education of Young Children
1834 Connecticut Avenue, NW
Washington, DC 20009

National Association for Mental Health
10 Columbus Circle
New York, NY 10019

National Association for Retarded Citizens
2501 Avenue J
Arlington, TX 76011

National Association of Private Schools for Exceptional Children
7700 Miller Road
Miami, FL 33155

National Association of Protection and Advocacy Systems
300 I Street NE
Suite 212
Washington, DC 20002

National Consortium for Child Mental Health Services
1424 Sixteenth Street, NW
Suite 201A
Washington, DC 20036

National Education Association
1201 Sixteenth Street, NW
Washington, DC 20036

National Easter Seal Society
2023 West Ogden Avenue
Chicago, IL 60612

National Information Center for Handicapped Children and Youth
1355 Wilson Boulevard
Rosslyn, VA 22209

National Institute of Mental Health
5454 Wisconsin Avenue
Chevy Chase, MD 20015

National Organization for Rare Disorders
P.O. Box 8923
New Fairfield, CT 06812

National Registry for Autism and Tourette's Syndrome
Autism Training Center
Marshall University
Old Main, Room 316
Huntington, WV 25755-2430

Special Education Parents Alliance
Suite K-164
305 22nd Street
Glen Ellyn, IL 60137

Professional periodicals.   The following magazines and journals are for both professionals and laypeople. Asterisks (*) designate periodicals that may be appropriate for the nonprofessional.

*The Advocate**
Exceptional Children
*Exceptional Parent**
Journal of Applied Behavior Analysis
Journal of the Association for Persons with Severe Handicaps
*Focus on Autistic Behavior**
Journal of Autism and Developmental Disorders

Videotapes.   The following videos deal with either general information, relationships, education, or behavior management. They may be rented or purchased. (Much of the list below was obtained from the Michigan Society for Autistic Citizens.)

Behavior Technology for Living and Working in the Community. Rockville, MD: CC-M Production for Community Services for Autistic Adults and Children
Teaching Social and Leisure Skills to Youth with Autism. Bloomington, IN: Indiana University Audio-Visual Center
Regular Lives. Washington, DC: State of the Art Production
Supportive Employment "It Works." Oklahoma State University: National University Telecommunications
With a Little Help From My Friends. Toronto, Canada: Vision Vidsomanic
Reaching the Child Within. Arlington, VA: PBS Video
They Don't Come with Manuals. Boston, MA: Fanlight Productions
Like an Ordinary Brother. University of Washington: Media Services Child Development and Mental Retardation Center
Special Kids, Special Dads. Vision Productions
Least Restrictive Environment. Bloomington, IN: Indiana University Audio-Visual Center
Almost Like You and Me. CC-M Productions, Inc.
Portrait of an Autistic Young Man. Los Angeles: Behavioral Sciences Media Laboratory
Autism: A World Apart. Boston, MA: Fanlight Productions

A New Way of Thinking. Minneapolis: Minnesota Universty Affiliated
Program on Developmental Disabilities
Autism: The Invisible Wall. Oklahoma City: University of Oklahoma
Medical Center

Books. The following books may be of interest to parents and
professionals:

Ellis, A., & Harper, R. A. (1979). *A new guide to rational living.* No. Holly-
wood, CA: Wilshire.
Greenfield, J. (1972). *A child called Noah.* New York: Holt, Reinhart &
Winston.
Greenfield, J. (1978). *A place for Noah.* New York: Holt, Reinhart &
Winston.
Kaufman, B. N. (1976). *Son-rise.* New York: Harper & Row.
Meyer, D. J., Vadasy, P. F., & Fewell, R. R. (1985). *Living with a brother or
sister with special needs: A book for sibs.* Seattle: University of Wash-
ington Press.
Morgan, S. B. (1981). *The unreachable child: An introduction to early
childhood autism.* Memphis, TN: Memphis State University Press.